Collins

English for Business

LISTENING

Ian Badger

Collins

HarperCollins Publishers
The News Building
1 London Bridge Street
London
SE1 9GF

First edition 2011

10 9 8 7 6 5 4

© HarperCollins Publishers 2011

ISBN 978–0–00–742321–7

Collins® is a registered trademark
of HarperCollins Publishers Limited

www.collinselt.com

A catalogue record for this book is available from
the British Library

Typeset by Davidson Publishing Solutions, Glasgow

Printed in China by RR Donnelley APS

DEDICATION & ACKNOWLEDGEMENTS

For Mum and Dad

I would especially like to thank:

– all who agreed to being recorded. We could not have done this without you!

– the HarperCollins team: Nikki McMullan, Catherine Whitaker, Celia Wigley and Holly Roper-Newman for their infectious support, encouragement and enthusiasm

– Teresa Miller from BMES, Bristol for her valuable comments and suggestions during the writing process

– Dominic O'Dwyer from Bristol University and Ian McMaster from Business Spotlight in Munich

– the UPM employees who listened to and gave feedback on the work-in-progress

About the author

Ian Badger is a highly regarded author who has written a wide range of published materials to aid spoken and written communication in English. He runs a training consultancy (BMES) which specialises in helping the employees of international companies to communicate with their counterparts, contacts, and customers worldwide. This work, which involves helping speakers from all over the world to communicate clearly and effectively with each other, has made him acutely aware of the need to understand English however it is spoken.

Ian is originally from London but now lives in Bristol in the west of England. He spends a lot of his time running face-to-face training in Finland, Germany, France, and Russia and working remotely in many other parts of the world. He has worked as a director of studies, teacher trainer, teacher of English, and communications consultant and is a regular speaker at international conferences.

Ian is also the author of *English for Life: Listening B1* (Collins 2012).

Contents

Introduction

Collins English for Business: Listening will improve your understanding of what your colleagues, customers, suppliers and other business contacts are saying in English.

You can use *Listening*:

- as a self-study course
- as supplementary material on a business communication or business English course.

Listening aims to develop your awareness and sensitivity to different accents. As you listen to the recordings, you will note which speakers are easier to follow and notice why this is the case: speed, clear accent, lack of complex vocabulary and idiom, straightforward use of grammar. By studying these features of other people's language, you will gain more awareness of your own English and take steps to ensure that you become a clearer speaker.

Specifically, *Listening* will help you to develop:

- listening for the gist/the main points made by speakers
- listening for the exact meaning of words and phrases
- awareness of clear usage and structures
- your range of business-related vocabulary
- cultural awareness

Listening comprises a **book** and **CD**. The **book** consists of 20 units divided into the following five sections:

1   Everyday business communication
2   Working internationally: some impressions
3   Outside the office
4   Everyday business matters
5   Cultural considerations

You can either work through the units from Unit 1 to Unit 20 or pick and choose the units that are most useful to you.

The **CD** contains 55 recordings of American, Chinese, Japanese, Indian, Italian, Spanish, British, Irish, French and Australian speakers among others. The ability to understand varieties of English is a key to better business performance and success.

At the back of the book there is:

- a mini-dictionary
- the answer key
- the transcripts for the audio recordings.

Using *Listening*

For ease of use, each unit follows a similar structure. It is recommended that you follow the order of exercises when working through a unit. Each unit includes:

- Some simple questions to check your understanding of what is said.
- Exercises which focus on extracts from the recording where you can check your understanding of specific features: pronunciation, vocabulary, structure.
- Gap-filling exercises intended to direct your attention to specific words and phrases which may cause comprehension problems.
- Vocabulary-matching exercises to widen your vocabulary. A poor vocabulary is often the reason that misunderstandings occur.

In some cases the language level of the exercises may appear low, but understanding the gist and details of the recordings will present a challenge.

Other features

'Powered by COBUILD'

In order to help you to extend your vocabulary, further uses of key language are explored through references to examples taken from the Collins COBUILD corpus. In addition, you can look up any unfamiliar words and phrases in the mini-dictionary at the back of the book. This contains definitions and further examples from the *Collins COBUILD Advanced Dictionary*.

Did you know?

Small sections set in speech bubbles provide useful background information which will help you to understand the context of a recording.

Clear usage

These sections focus on specific issues which can cause problems for the listener, such as complex grammar forms used by native speakers or non-standard usage.

Further study

The final section in the each unit provides you with some suggestions for further study. In most cases it refers you to complimentary listening material on the *Listening* website: **www.collinselt.com/businesslistening**.

We all make mistakes!

'Since many years I haven't seen a rifle in your hand!' From Fernando, *ABBA*

Native and very fluent non-native speakers make 'mistakes' – even ABBA. The recordings that accompany *Listening* were recorded on location (i.e. not in a studio) and are unscripted. As happens in the real world, the speakers make mistakes. They sometimes use unconventional grammar forms, they do not always speak in full sentences, and they hesitate regularly. These real 'errors' have not been removed from the recordings. The speakers' views are also unscripted and reflect their individual opinions and knowledge.

Language level

Listening has been written to help business learners at B1 level and above (Intermediate to Advanced).

Other titles

Also available in the *Collins English for Business* series: *Speaking* and *Writing*

Using the CD

This icon indicates that there is an audio track that you should listen to. Please note that the *Listening* CD is designed for use with a computer. If you want to play the audio on a CD player, you should download the tracks to your computer and then burn all of the tracks onto an audio CD.

1 Communicating clearly

Think like a wise man, but communicate in the language of the people.
– William Butler Yeats (Irish poet and dramatist)

A

Seamus is from Northern Ireland. In this recording, he discusses features of his Northern Irish English and how he has become 'anglicised' in his efforts to make himself clearly understood.

1 **Read the general comprehension questions below. Then, play track 1 through once and answer the questions.**

1 What feature of Seamus's English does he mention as causing some comprehension problems?

2 What feature of his pronunciation does he identify as helping people to understand him particularly well?

3 How has he modified his language in order to make himself more easily understood?

4 How long does it usually take him to revert to his Irish accent when he goes home?

2 **Now listen again. As you play the recording, familiarise yourself with the way Seamus pronounces the words and phrases which are underlined.**

– OK, well I'll talk to you <u>later.</u>

– This is really <u>something</u> very specific to do with the <u>nature</u> of my local English accent from Northern <u>Ireland</u>.

– You don't need a road <u>map</u> to get <u>around</u> – you need a <u>score</u>.

– People say I speak very <u>clearly</u>.

– … in the way that I <u>pronounce</u> words.

'The score'

Seamus says: 'There's a joke in my home town that you don't need a road map to get around – you need the score.'

He is referring to the 'sing-song' style of the Derry accent, which is said to be like a musical score.

Derry (also knows as Londonderry) is the second-largest city in Northern Ireland.

---

3 Now listen again, stop the recording as necessary, and complete the gaps in the sentences.

1 I would never accept that I'm .... except Northern Irish.
2 I think the accent has ....
3 I speak with quite a .... intonation.
4 We don't drop the .... as in Received Pronunciation.
5 I think the .... are quite round.
6 I've slowed .... down quite considerably.
7 When I go back home, people say I've become extremely ....
8 After about three hours it speeds up again [...] sort of .... to type.

Clear usage: I have changed ('I've' changed)

Note the way Seamus discusses how **he has changed** the way he speaks in order to get his message across more clearly. Notice also how he contracts *I have* to *I've*.

'When I've said, 'OK, well I'll talk to you later' ...'

'I've actually modified the way I speak.'

'I've slowed the speed of delivery.'

'I've become extremely anglicised.'

---

4 Match the verbs in the left hand column, which are taken from the recording, with words on the right which have similar meanings.

1 mellow   a say
2 drop   b stop
3 pronounce   c soften
4 pause   d adapt
5 modify   e return
6 revert   f leave out

B

In this next recording, Seamus continues to describe how he modifies his language in order to communicate clearly.

1 Read the comprehension questions below. Then, play the recording through once and answer the questions.

1 What did Seamus consider to be most important when communicating in export markets?
2 What is his attitude towards the use of incorrect grammar?
3 What is more important in his view – having knowledge of the product or having the ability to communicate clearly?
4 What was the most important lesson he learnt in his first year of business?

2 Now listen again, pause the recording when necessary, and complete the following phrases.

1 After my first .... working in the export market.

2 If that meant .... the way that I speak to make it easier for people to understand me, then that's what I would do.

3 I avoid more .... in sentences.

4 I occasionally will speak incorrect grammar just to .... across.

5 Depending on, of course, the language skills of the person .... to.

6 That's the most .... of the job.

7 You're already up against a ....

8 So .... is by far the most important thing I learnt.

Clear usage: subjunctives and subordinate clauses

Seamus says:

'I would leave out subjunctive clauses and subordinate clauses.'

The **subjunctive** mood of a verb is used to express wishes, hopes, doubts, etc. It is not often used in English but here are some examples:

I recommend that this <u>be</u> organised later. (present subjunctive)

I recommend that we should organise this later. (avoiding the subjunctive)

<u>Were we</u> to organise this, how much would it cost? (past subjunctive)

If we organised this, how much would it cost? (avoiding the subjunctive)

A **subordinate clause** is the part of a sentence which is less important than the main part of a sentence – a subordinate clause cannot stand on its own. Some examples (the subordinate clause is underlined):

<u>Having made the decision</u>, he ended the meeting.

<u>When I get to the station</u>, I am going to get something to eat.

I spoke to our agent, <u>who is Egyptian</u>, about the new office procedures.'

C

In this recording, Jude, who is from the south of England, talks about the respect that she has for those who have to do business in English when it is not their native language; she goes on to talk about a specific experience of communicating in English in the UAE.

1 Read the comprehension questions below. Then, play the recording through once and answer the questions. Do not worry about understanding every word and phrase.

1 What was a challenge for Jude?

2   What was the situation she mentions when the 'shoe was on the other foot'?

3   What is Jude's key consideration when writing emails internationally?

4   Why was it occasionally difficult for Jude to understand Indian speakers of English when she was working in the UAE?

 2 **Now listen again, stop the recording as necessary, and complete the gaps in the sentences.**

1   From my ……………………………………………, I just had to explain things as clearly as possible …

2   … and just remember, ……………………………………………, that these people are writing …

3   But ……………… working internationally is just sort of bearing in mind that …

4   There were lots of ………………………… living in the UAE.

5   In fact, ……………… of the population was Indian in that area.

6   … which I'd have to ……………… them to explain.

⋐ COBUILD CHECK: the language of language

- *He spoke with a pronounced Southern **accent** in a high-pitched nasal voice.*

- *His **accent** was so thick and so impenetrable that much of what he said had to be repeated.*

- *If we wish to pronounce a language well, we must reproduce its sound, its rhythm and its **intonation** as accurately as possible.*

- *The local **dialect** is almost unintelligible to anyone arriving from the capital.*

- *Although speakers of a language understand **idioms**, their meanings are not predictable from the words used in the expression.*

- *She used **acronyms** and terms that were completely alien to me.*

- *OK, O.K., okay: all three spellings are acceptable, but avoid this **colloquial** term in formal speech and writing.*

- *His 'Oxford accent' (or **Received Pronunciation**, RP) is considered by some as elite and posh; by others as the clearest and best way of speaking.*

FURTHER STUDY

For further recordings of Seamus and Jude, go to the website **www.collinselt.com/businesslistening.**

2

Understanding different accents in English

I don't want to lose my accent; I just want it to become smaller.
– Goran Visnjic (Croatian actor who lives and works in the USA)

A

Kara is from New York and works in international sales. In this recording, she discusses which accents she finds easy to understand and which she finds difficult.

1 **Read the comprehension questions below. Then, play the recording through once and answer the questions.**

1 Why does Kara find it difficult to understand every word spoken by those who consider themselves to be fluent speakers of English?

2 In which of the countries in which she works does she find it easiest to use English?

3 Why does she find it difficult to understand Nigerian speakers of English?

4 How does she feel after a day of speaking to Nigerian speakers?

2 **Now listen again. Notice the way that Kara pronounces the following words and expressions. Note in particular how she pronounces key vowel sounds: *ha̱rd*, *ve̱ry*, *spea̱k/rea̱d*, *o̱f*, *Yo̱rk* and *la̱nguage/ima̱gine/Fra̱nce*.**

– Some of the accents, as a native English speaker, I still find quite difficult.

– It's extremely hard to get every word.

– I feel very rude in meetings.

– They all speak and read in English.

– They only have about two or three shelves in each bookstore of their own native language.

– … in my old position in New York […] That's their official language.

– I can't imagine, if someone from France is speaking in English to someone from Nigeria speaking in English, …

Useful vocabulary and phrases: checking understanding

Excuse me, I didn't catch that.

Sorry, could you say that again?

Could you spell that?

Could you speak up (a bit)?

Could you say that again more slowly, please?

Sorry, what did you say about Tagalog?

Did you say Haye or Hayes?

Did you say you were coming on Tuesday or Thursday?

Just to check, could you put that in an email?

Clear usage: used to

Kara says:

'I used to work with a lot of Nigerian customers.'

The use of the construction 'used to' implies that Kara *no longer* has any Nigerian customers but *at one time* she spent a lot of time working with them. Here are some other expressions for talking about past experiences using 'used to':

Unfortunately, I didn't use to travel to there very often.

I really used to enjoy spending time with my Nigerian colleagues.

When I was younger, I used to spend a lot of time travelling in the Middle East.

Note that 'would' can be used as an alternative to 'used to':

We would often eat out together in the evenings.

I usually wouldn't get home to my hotel until late.

In those 17 years that I worked in that company, I would travel over to Shanghai two or three times a year.

Nigerian English

English is an official language in Nigeria so the level of English spoken by Nigerians is high. However, to the unaccustomed ear (such as Kara's), the Nigerian accent is strong, and there are many interesting English expressions that don't exist outside Nigeria.

Not on seat. = Away from the office / Not in the office.

Me a go tell dem. = I'm going to tell them.

Make we ... = Let's ...

We dey foh Lagos. = We are in Lagos.

to rub minds = to brainstorm

More grease to your elbow! = Well done!

 3 For intensive listening practice, now listen again. Stop the recording as necessary and complete the gaps in the sentences.

1 I feel very rude in meetings sometimes .... saying, 'Excuse me?'

2 Would you mind .... that?

3 My ear has .... better at the various accents.

4 I .... work with a lot of Nigerian customers.

5 But it's such a quick, ... English.

6 After a full day of meetings, you feel so ....

B Gayatri is from Kashmir in the far north of India. In this recording, she discusses the diversity of accents in India.

 1 Read the comprehension questions below. Then, play the recording through once and answer the questions.

1 Approximately how many official languages are there in India?

2 What two factors does Gayatri mention as affecting Indian people's accent?

3 How easy does Gayatri think it is to tell from an Indian person's accent which region he or she is from?

4 How easy does she think it is to tell which region in India she is from?

2 **Now listen again. Notice the way that Gayatri pronounces the following words and expressions. She does not have a strong accent. Do you find it easy to understand her?**

   – India's a very diverse land.

   – … people from Punjab have a different accent, people from Kashmir have a very different accent …

   – … so it's very, very diverse.

   – It really depends on whether they have that regional accent or not.

   – if I were to come across somebody from my region.

3 **Listen again. Stop the recording as necessary and complete the gaps in the sentences.**

   1 On our currency .... twenty-four times.

   2 Based on different regions, the accents .... as well.

   3 Sometimes you can .... if an Indian person is from a certain region.

   4 You can lose the .... accent.

   5 I might .... my regional accent.

   6 But .... that, no.

C

Rohit is also from India, from Bangalore. He has regular contact in English worldwide. In this short recording, he discusses the problems that he has when working in English with non-native speakers of English.

1 **Read the comprehension questions below. Then, play the track through once and answer the questions.**

   1 When is it more difficult for Rohit to conduct business in English?

   2 Apart from different accents, what else causes Rohit comprehension problems?

3   What has he learned to do in order to communicate effectively in English?

2   **Listen again. Stop the recording as necessary, and complete the gaps in the sentences.**

1   [A] lot of us in India are .... speakers.

2   If you work with somebody in ....
.... guy.

3   You have people who don't .... speak English.

4   You ...., you know, read between the lines.

5   That's the other .... of working globally in English.

Varieties of English ·

Gayatri talks about the varieties of English that exist in India alone. There are many books available which explore in depth the subject of 'world English'. This is a quote from *International English: A guide to the varieties of Standard English* by P. Trudgill and J. Hannah, Hodder Education 2008 (Indian English pp 133-139):

"English is an official language in India and is used as one of the languages of education and wider communication. There are a number of native speakers of English in India, but these are far outnumbered by those for whom it is an additional language… The pronunciation of Indian English varies quite considerably depending on the speaker's native language as well as on his or her educational background and degree of exposure to native English."

---

3   **Rohit talks about how both accent and unfamiliar grammar can cause problems in communicating globally in English. What do you consider to be the greatest barriers to your clear communication? If you work with American or Indian speakers of English, ask them if you can record your conversations and then analyse them. How do the speakers in these recordings compare with the American and Indian speakers you have heard?**

FURTHER STUDY

For some additional recordings, go to
www.collinselt.com/businesslistening.

3 Conference calls

We have two ears and one mouth so that we can listen twice as much as we speak. – Epictetus (Greek philosopher)

A

Conference calls often involve going through an automated service. The caller must follow instructions in order to be connected to their call. In this first recording you will hear the initial part of a conference call – the log-in procedure and introductions from the participants.

 1 Read the comprehension questions below. Then, play the recording through once and answer the questions.

1 During the log-in procedure the participant must enter a code plus which key?
2 Is the participant successful when she first tries to log in? Why not?
3 What does the participant need to do if she needs technical assistance during the call?
4 What is the total number of participants in the conference call?
5 What is the weather like where Lorna is calling in from?

Useful vocabulary and phrases: telephone and computer commands

Press the hash key (#) (*known in US English as 'the pound key'*) / the star key (*)

Hold down the Ctrl / Control key whilst pressing F4

Go to the drop-down menu and click on 'Properties'

It's below the Windows toolbar

Scroll down until you come to …

It's in the top left hand corner of your screen

It's in the bottom right hand corner

Check the box / Uncheck the box

---

 2 Now listen again, stop the recording as necessary and complete the gaps in the sentences. Note the particular form of UK native-speaker small talk at the beginning of this conference call:

1 At any time during this message ……………… your participant pass code.
2 The pass code you are attempting to enter – three, three, eight, three, eight, three, five, two – ……………… .
3 Thank you. Your pass code ………………………………… .
4 If you are a participant, you may hear music until the leader……………… the conference.
5 It's a lovely day down here today – ……………… for yesterday, really.
6 Certainly it was ……………… by the time I'd got out to the car today.

Clear usage: a conference call

Note the colloquial phrases used by native English speakers in track 7's extract from a conference call:

'Hi, guys'; 'Hello'; 'Hi'; 'Hi, Nigel. How are you?' (informal greetings at the beginning of the call)

'Edmund here'; 'This is Nigel' (alternative ways of announcing you have joined the conference)

'Good weekend?' (Shortened colloquial greeting alternative to *Did you have a good weekend?* or *How was your weekend?*)

'Is Nigel on?' (Has Nigel joined the call?)

'We've got Alex in/on the call' (Either 'in' or 'on' is correct here)

'OK, then. Edmund, do you want to take us through your highlight report, please?' (The speaker could also say: *Could you take us through...? / Please take us through...? / So, Edmund, take us through...?*)

B

This next conference call took place over the Internet, with both parties using an Internet calling service to talk to one another. The participants in this call are: Anna from Glasgow in Scotland and Rohit and Eddie from Bangalore in India. This recording covers the final part of their conference call. Some small sections are difficult to understand as the telephone line drops – something which can often happen in international calls.

 1 Read the comprehension questions below. Then, play the recording through once and answer the questions.

1 When will Alex be back from holiday?

2 What does Alex need to double-check when he gets back from holiday?

3 What did Bill say to Anna when she spoke to him?

4 What action had Rohit and Eddie taken concerning the missing information?

5 What action is Anna going to take to find the missing information?

 2 Listen to the recording again and note down the order in which the following phrases appear.

1 they should be processed already

2 he thought that we had everything

3 please let me know

4 that was still outstanding

5 quite a long time ago

6 Anna, another question

7 just to get that handed over

8 If I forward— bounce that back to you

3							

> Rohit says: 'What is the status on that?'
> This phrase is often used in projects to check on progress, for example:
> *Is a job waiting for a decision?*
> *What stage has it reached?*
> *Has it been completed?*

Useful vocabulary and phrases: dealing with a bad connection

Sorry, I didn't catch that.

Could you say that again?

I didn't catch your first name.

What did you say your surname was?
    (*'your last name' in US English*).

I lost you. Could you repeat that?

This is a very bad connection. I keep losing you.

I'll put the phone down and call you again.

Can you hear me better now?

Yes, that's much better.

No that's even worse!

3 Now listen again, stop the recording as necessary and complete the gaps in the sentences.

1 If you've got any .... in the meantime …

2 We know that there's a couple of .... invoices.

3 He's .... that they've forwarded everything on.

4 We just sent back an email .... what is missing.

5 I'll .... if I've still got that email.

6 I think I .... to Bill …

7 You can confirm that that's still .... Then we can chase up.

> Anna says: 'We know that there's a couple of …'
> 'Standard' usage would be: *We know that there are a couple of …*

⊟ COBUILD CHECK: conducting business on the telephone

- Many people telephoning a large company with a **query** will have experienced being passed around from extension to extension.

- They **double-check** everything relating to telephone orders for accuracy and clarity.

- While investors and analysts often participate in management **conference calls**, most security holders do not participate in these calls.

- Managers at the new factory in Alabama hold a two-hour **teleconference** with head office in Stuttgart every week.

- Any further **hold-up** would upset the schedule of the project, which is due to finish in April.

- He telephoned the company and then sent an email **outlining** the programme details.

- I spent many hours on the phone **chasing up** agencies and responding to job ads.

- A number of **outstanding** issues still remain to be resolved.

5 tips for a better telephone conference

1 Prepare an agenda that clearly sets out the objectives for the meeting and include timings if appropriate. Ask participants to make sure that they read through the agenda before the call.

2 Ensure that all participants have the dial-in number and any pass codes needed (including international country codes and information about toll-free numbers).

3 Consider the impact of time zones when planning your meeting.

4 Establish a clear etiquette for the conference covering conventions for joining and leaving, interrupting, allowing time for 'break-out' time, summarising.

5 Speak as clearly as possible. In many cases this will mean slowing down. This is particularly important if you have an accent which your colleagues find difficult to understand.

Which tips of your own would you add to this list?

4 **Match the words on the left, taken from the recording, with the words on the right which have similar meanings.**

1	query	a	position
2	holdup	b	question
3	status	c	write
4	compose	d	delay
5	highlight	e	deal with
6	process	f	stress

FURTHER STUDY

Scottish and Indian accents can both be challenging to understand if you do not hear them often. For further recordings of Indian and Scottish speakers of English, go to **www.collinselt.com/businesslistening.**

4 Voicemails

Please leave a message after the beep!

A   This unit consists of a number of voicemails. The first two voicemails are left by Catrina, who is Canadian, and Nick, who is English.

1   Read the comprehension questions below. Then, play the recording through once and answer the questions.

1   Which meeting is Catrina calling about?
2   What is the problem?
3   What is she going to have to do about the meeting?
4   When would Catrina like to reschedule the meeting for?

Useful vocabulary and phrases: changing arrangements

I'm sorry* but I can't make the meeting.

I'm afraid* we'll have to reschedule it.

Something urgent has come up.

I'm going to have to reschedule.

We'll need to find another time.

I'd really appreciate it if we could push our meeting back by an hour.

This week is really busy – would you mind if we moved it off to next week?

When are you free next week?

* Note that it is common in English to use '(I'm) sorry but' and 'I'm afraid' before suggesting changes, giving unwelcome news, etc.

Misleading expressions of time

Time expressions which can cause misunderstandings:

I'll call you **next** *Thursday* (not this Thursday)

next Thursday = Thursday next week

this Thursday = Thursday this week

half four = 4.30 *(colloquial)*.

---

2   Now listen again, stop the recording as necessary and complete the gaps in the sentences.

1   It's Catrina ....
2   I'm .... calling about the meeting we have scheduled.
3   ...., I have another meeting.
4   I'm gonna .... reschedule for another time.
5   If you could give me .... back ...
6   ... I'd really .... it.

10

3 In track 10, Nick explains why he is going to be late for a meeting. Play the track through once and answer these general comprehension questions.

1 What time is Nick's meeting?

2 What is he doing when he calls?

3 How long does he think the rest of his journey will take?

4 How late does he expect to be?

Note that Nick says: 'I'm sat on the M25 doing no miles an hour!'
The M25 is a motorway that runs around London.
'I'm sat' (colloquial) = *I'm sitting* = *I'm not moving*
'Doing no miles an hour' = *I'm at a standstill*

Useful vocabulary and phrases: informing a colleague of a delay

I'm running a little late.

The train is running two hours late.

I hope to be with you in half an hour.

I'm at the airport and the flight is delayed.

We haven't taken off yet.

The traffic is terrible.

I'm stuck in traffic.

I'll call you as soon as I arrive at the station.

I'll let you know as soon as we land.

Sorry about this, but there's nothing I can do!

10

4 Now listen again, stop the recording as necessary, and complete the gaps in the sentences.

1 Hi, it's Nick. .... sorry.

2 I know we've got an ....

3 ...but (I'm) .... sat on the M25.

4 You know my ....

5 Give me .... if you need to speak to me.

B The next two voicemails are left by Chinese speakers of English.

11

1 Yue has left some instructions about how to get to the centre of Beijing from the airport. Play the recording through once. Are these statements true or false?

	True	False
1 She recommends taking the Airport Express to the city centre.		
2 She already knows where her colleague is staying.		
3 She recommends getting off at Tiananmen station.		
4 She strongly recommends taking a taxi to the hotel.		

2 Listen to the way Yue pronounces the following. Underline any words and phrases which you find difficult to understand. Compare your pronunciation with hers.

- If you want to get from the airport to (the) downtown …
- There are a lot of lines.
- One line will go to Xidan.
- If your hotel is in Tiananmen …
- You can get down when the bus came [comes] to (the) Tiananmen.
- And you can go to your hotel by taxi or by bus, by subway.

3 Yuting was supposed to meet her colleague Peter at the airport but leaves a message to say that he should make his own way to the office. Answer the questions to check that you have understood the message.

1 Why can't Yuting meet Peter?
2 What does she suggest as the best way of getting to the office?
3 Where does she suggest that they should meet?

4 Listen for the following words and note down in which order they appear.

1	district	5	sorry
2	taxi	6	station
3	since	7	entrance
4	next to	8	now

5 ☐ ☐ ☐ ☐ ☐ ☐ ☐

C

This voicemail is left by Jindee, who is from Bangkok in Thailand. She is telling her colleague how to get to her office.

1 Read the comprehension questions below. Then, play the recording through once and answer the questions.

1 How does she recommend that he gets to the skytrain station?
2 What does Jindee think she's forgotten?
3 Which bus should he take to the office?
4 What is the alternative that she suggests?

Note that Jindee says: 'You just easily by walk to the main road.'

'Standard' usage would be: *It is easy to walk to the main road* or *You can easily walk to the main road.*

Jindee says: 'Then you take off.'

'Standard' usage would be: *Then you get off.*

Useful vocabulary and phrases: directions

Take any bus in the direction of the centre – the driver will tell you when to get off.

Take the shuttle bus from the airport to the main station.

You'll need to buy a ticket before you board the train.

You'll have to change trains at Hamm.

If I remember correctly, you have to change platforms.

If you're driving, take the E12 until you get to Palkane and then follow the signs to Valkeakoski.

Take the M4 motorway until junction 19. Follow the M32 into the centre of town. Cross a roundabout and you will see our office on the right hand side.

If you have any problems, just call me.

Differences between UK and US English

UK English	US English
city centre	downtown
motorway	interstate/highway
junction (*motorway*)	exit
junction (*crossroads*)	intersection
roundabout	traffic circle
turn right	turn right / take a right (*colloquial*)

13

2 **Now listen again, stop the recording as necessary, and complete the gaps in the sentences.**

1 I'm sorry I cannot .... today.

2 Then you may .... the bus if you want to.

3 Just tell them the .... name.

4 They will .... you there.

5 It's not too ....

FURTHER STUDY

To listen to more voicemail messages, go online to **www.collinselt.com/businesslistening.**

5

USA and Canada

I like to listen. I have learned a great deal from listening carefully.
Most people never listen. – Ernest Hemingway (American author)

A

Chris is from North Dakota in the United States. In this recording he talks about differences in everyday business life in different parts of the US.

1 Read the comprehension questions below. Then, play the recording through once and answer the questions.

1 Where did Sam Walton, the founder of Walmart, open his first corner shop?

2 What was Chris's impression of visiting Walmart's Head Office?

3 Which city did Chris visit last on his business trip?

4 How would Chris characterise life in Manhattan?

2 Read aloud the phrases below. Then listen to Chris's pronunciation of them. Compare your pronunciation with his.

– We do a lot of business with Walmart

– The single biggest retailer in the world.

– … based out of what is a Podunk, quite rural little town.

– On my last business trip there, I came straight from Manhattan.

– It's a real shock to the system.

– It was interesting to see the different lifestyle things going on.

– San Diego just seemed to be about getting outside.

– And Seattle was— we drank a lot of coffee!

A 'Podunk' town

Chris jokingly describes Bentonville as a 'Podunk' town. When asked to define 'Podunk', which is not a familiar term outside the States, he replies: 'Podunk?
Podunk is probably from the 40s but it means a small, one-horse, quite rural town, a bit of a backwater. It can be used in kind of a derogatory way, but often it's just a way of indicating that something's rural and small. A Podunk town is just like my town in North Dakota, where I grew up, so I feel as though I can say that!'

3 Now listen again, stop the recording as necessary and complete the gaps in the sentences.

1 A little .... town in Arkansas.

2 An airport that's .... by Walmart for the town.

3 You probably don't necessarily give them the same sort of (oh gosh) ...., stance, attitude.

4 It was relaxing, ... and probably works to their favour.

5 Suddenly, ... from winter-summer, then I went back up for the winter in Seattle.

4 Now listen one more time. Notice how Chris uses a lot of 'fillers' in his speech to give himself 'thinking time'. Underline the words and phrases you hear him use.

I think	well
it's kind of	you know
I suppose	basically
I have to say	I reckon
it's like	I mean
sort of	you probably

B Tonya lives in Atlanta in Georgia, USA, but she grew up on a farm in North Carolina. Here, she talks about the differences in the US between working in a city and working in the countryside.

1 Read the comprehension questions below. Then, play the recording through once and answer the questions.

1 Where does Tonya believe that you can find a stronger work ethic – in the city or in a rural location?

2 How does the pace of work compare in the city and the countryside?

3 Where does Tonya prefer to live – in the city or on the farm?

2 Read aloud the following phrases, all taken from Tonya's recording, and then listen to Tonya again. Compare your pronunciation with hers. Do you notice any differences when comparing the way she speaks with the way Chris speaks?

– I think there are differences in work ethic and culture.

– The 'go-go-go' mentality of living in the city.

– A farm requires a great deal of work.

– They still get all the work done – just at a little slower pace.

– I'm in Atlanta, Georgia.

– I have to tell you, I prefer the hustle and bustle!

- *Rural Minnesota is far from the **hustle and bustle** of big cities like New York and Los Angeles, geographically and spiritually.*

- *The residents have not yet lost their old-fashioned sense of hospitality and **laid-back** lifestyle.*

- *Increasingly, developers are turning to **smartening up** existing malls rather than building new ones.*

- *With its often treeless landscape and slow-moving streams, this is generally regarded as a sleepy rural **backwater**.*

- *There are over 70 universities and colleges in the Boston **metropolitan** area, including world-famous Harvard University.*

- *Nowadays our homes need to be a sanctuary from the frantic **pace** of life.*

Clear usage: 'getting things done'

Tonya says:
'They still get all the work done.'

Other examples:

> *Did you manage to get everything done yesterday?*
> *I'm hoping to get the work done by the end of the day.*
> *I'm sorry but I won't get it done until tomorrow.*
> *If you can't get it done by the deadline, please let me know immediately.*

C

Catrina is from Toronto in Canada. She has also lived in Ottawa and Montreal, which, she says, accounts for her 'slightly random Canadian accent'. In this short recording, she gives some impressions of differences between the USA and Canada.

16

1 **Read the following questions. Then, play the recording through once and answer the questions to check your general comprehension.**

1 How similar is the 'American heritage' to the 'Canadian heritage'?

2 In Catrina's view, how do Canadians feel about their links with the United Kingdom?

3 How does she think that Americans and Canadians compare in terms of their attitudes to work?

16

2 **Now listen to the recording again and complete the gaps in the following sentences.**

1 I mean, popular culture is .... between the two countries.

2 Half of the biggest Canadian stars most people .... are Canadian.

3 The Canadian heritage is quite .... the American heritage.

4   I think Canadians are .... of their link to England.

5   All of that history is quite .... in being Canadian.

6   You know, it's a .... nation.

7   It's a much ...., quieter kind of way of life.

8   Americans .... quite 'go-go-go'.

3   **Divide the following words into two groups, depending on whether they refer to behaviour which is *relaxed* or *not relaxed*.**

laid-back	calm	go-go-go	frenetic	hectic	chaotic
tranquil	demanding	frantic	quiet	busy	peaceful

Relaxed   **Not relaxed**

....

....

....

....

....

....

....

⊑ COBUILD CHECK: working culture

- *I have become a total **workaholic**, and this can put a major strain on family, relationships, and social life.*

- *Both sides have been **embroiled** in a labour dispute for more than a year.*

- *Contemporary workplace **culture** demands people demonstrate their dedication through longer days.*

- *Aggressive behaviour threatens, punishes, or **puts down** other people.*

- *Right now, the situation is so **fluid** it's premature to make any kind of prediction.*

- *In addition to attending college, they both have part-time jobs to help offset the costs of their **go-go-go** lifestyles.*

Chris, Tonya and Catrina use words such as 'workaholicky' and 'go-go-go' to illustrate the fast pace which they observe in American business life. These are words that you might not find in a dictionary but they are perfectly acceptable when they are spoken.

FURTHER STUDY

For further recordings of Chris, Tonya and Catrina, go to the website **www.collinselt.com/businesslistening.**

6 Ireland and Germany

The single biggest problem in communication is the illusion that it has taken place. – George Bernard Shaw (Irish playwright)

A

Graham is from Dublin in Ireland and is currently working in financial recruitment in England. In this recording he makes some observations on English and Irish business culture.

1 Read the following questions, then play the recording through once. Answer the questions to check your general comprehension.

1 What does Graham see as a prerequisite for doing business in Ireland?

2 What has been the response of potential English business clients when Graham has offered to take them out for lunch before doing any business with them?

3 How would his English business clients feel about Irish 'familiarity' at the very beginning of a business relationship?

⊜ COBUILD CHECK: building business relationships

- *The company believes that appropriate hospitality is an important way of **getting to know** and understand our customers better.*

- *Their way of life is totally **alien** to the way in which I was brought up and the values I was taught to believe in.*

- *When we are **overly** sensitive to criticism, we take it more personally than professionally.*

- *He admitted that he was **taken aback** when he learned how his staff viewed him.*

- *It seemed mean to press him on a point he was obviously **reluctant** to discuss.*

---

2 Now listen again, stop the recording as necessary, and complete the gaps in the sentences.

1 Irish culture's mostly about ....

2 It's a lot about who you know, who .... are.

3 You'll find a lot of Irish people are .... to do business with people who ...

4 There's this .... of getting to know potential customers.

5 ... which is .... to people here.

6 I've often done it, when trying to .... with a new client, ...

7 No, that's something we do when ...., not before we begin.

B

Owen is from Dublin in the Republic of Ireland but has been working in Germany for a number of years. In this recording he is asked to summarise the difference between doing business in Ireland and in Germany. If you are familiar with these two countries, do you share his views?

 1 Read the questions below, then play the recording through once. Answer the questions for general comprehension.

1 Does Owen think the 'hierarchical system' which exists in Germany also exists in Ireland?

2 How 'flexible and liberal' does he think the German Government is towards business?

3 Is it expensive to employ staff in Germany?

4 What is the effect of Government legislation on small companies who want to start up in Germany?

 2 Read the following phrases aloud and then listen to the way Owen pronounces them. Are there any words which you find particularly difficult to understand? Compare your pronunciation with his.

– It's chalk and cheese.

– How shall I say it?

– It's 'jobs for the boys' culture.

– They'll do you a favour; you'll do them a favour.

– There's a hierarchical system in Germany that simply doesn't exist in Ireland.

– Hiring people is very easy; firing people is very easy.

– The government tends to let businesses go and do what they want.

⊜ **COBUILD CHECK: some idiomatic expressions**

● As any company that has recently launched a brand should know, two customers can be as different as **chalk and cheese**. (= completely different)

● He also aims to attract slot machine players, the **bread and butter** (= the most important part/the part that provides the main income) of gambling revenues.

● But the biggest expense – the one that will **make or break** (= result in great success or total failure) far-offshore wind power – will probably be maintenance.

● Seasonal **ups and downs** (= a mixture of good and bad) are still the norm, and the current quarter is a traditional 'up' one for demand.

---

 3 Now listen again, stop the recording as necessary, and complete the gaps in the sentences.

1 Business in Germany is very ....

2 Laws in doing business are almost ....

3 Setting up small businesses is .... easy.

4 It's very .... and it's very liberal.

5 It's extraordinarily .... and difficult to do anything.

6　The economic costs of hiring someone as a full-time employee are
....

7　The difficulties of setting up businesses (are ...) really .... the growth of small businesses.

8　There's far more control and .... here in Germany.

⊜ COBUILD CHECK: useful expressions for recessionary times

- When a company wishes to **raise capital** from the stock market it issues a prospectus.

- We are increasingly concerned that this economic **downturn** is threatening to turn into a full recession.

- Last year, despite the **recession**, overall French cheese consumption grew.

- The 3G adventure got off to a bad start in Europe by nearly **bankrupting** the industry.

- The costs involved are **astronomical** and we are only a small independent charitable organisation.

- The company I was working for went into **liquidation** and that put me on the dole in December.

Clear usage: 'if' conditionals

Owen says:

'They'll do you a favour; you'll do them a favour.'

This expression is similar in meaning to the colloquial phrase, *You scratch my back, I'll scratch yours.*

Some more standard conditional forms with 'if':

They'll do you a favour if you do them a favour.

If you call me tomorrow, I'll make sure that I have all the documents ready.

If you send me the bill, I'll settle it immediately.

I'll check that everything is OK with the suppliers if you send me all the contact details.

Jobs for the boys

Owen talks about a 'jobs for the boys' culture. This involves showing favouritism to friends and acquaintances when making job appointments. The phrase is said to originate from the 'old boys network' from exclusive British public (i.e. private – not run by the state) schools. Compare with 'nepotism' which is favouritism shown to relatives and friends.

4　Match the words taken from the recording of Owen (1–8) with words which have an opposite meaning (a–h).

1	hierarchical	a	affordable
2	straightforward	b	non-hierarchical
3	extraordinary	c	liberal
4	astronomical	d	complicated
5	strict	e	rigid
6	stable	f	commonplace
7	flexible	g	insignificant
8	important	h	insecure

C

Giancarlo is a Peruvian currently working in Germany. In this short recording he makes some comparisons between everyday business life in Peru and Germany.

1 Read the comprehension questions below. Then, play the recording through once and answer the questions.

1 Do Peruvians usually eat first or talk business first?

2 In which country are business relationships 'warmer'?

3 In which country does Giancarlo think it is easier to do business?

2 Now listen again, stop the recording as necessary, and complete the gaps in the sentences.

1 In Peru (it) is very informal ....

2 If you wanna [= want to] talk about business, you go (to) ....

3 In Germany it's more ... it's colder, the way the people .... each other.

4 On ...., in Peru (you ...) it's just very, very hard to get something.

5 Here it's .... just to make business.

6 In Peru is more like you make, like, ...

7 In the end you don't .... what you want.

> Note that Giancarlo, in common with many native speakers of Spanish, does not pronounce the 'it' in sentences such as:
> 'Here **it** is more like you just talk about business.'
> 'In Germany **it** is colder.'
> 'In Peru **it** is more like you make circles.'

FURTHER STUDY

The focus here is on just two European countries and you may have contacts in others. Find out more about the culture, language and geography of your contact countries by doing research on the internet. Ask your colleagues in Europe if they would agree to you recording your conversations with them so that you can analyse what they say.

For further recordings of European speakers of English, go to **www.collinselt.com/businesslistening.**

7 India

When all other means of communication fail, try words! - Anon

A

Gayatri, from Kashmir in Northern India, is currently working in London. In this recording, she gives some advice to those who have yet to visit India.

1 Read the comprehension questions below. Then, play the recording through once and answer the questions.

1 'I would like them to see India the way it is.' According to Gayatri, what kind of country is India?

2 In Gayatri's opinion, what have multinational companies contributed to India's development?

3 How does Gayatri define the Indian working culture?

2 Now listen to Gayatri again. According to what she says, which of the following statements are true and which are false?

	True	False
1 India is a very diverse country.		
2 The corporate sector has made a great difference to Indian society.		
3 People are leaving the country because they believe their talents are not being used.		
4 Indians tend to work hard and go to bed early.		

3 Now listen again and this time think about Gayatri's pronunciation. Gayatri speaks very clear English. Do you have any difficulties understanding her pronunciation of the following words and phrases?

- I would like them to see India the way it is.
- … just like India has different terrains.
- We have from the most barren to the most lush terrain.
- That's the impression they're going to get when they go there.
- Most people don't really want to leave their home country.
- Life doesn't stop if you finish work at nine-thirty.
- They would get to see different kinds of food and culture.

Doing business in India

When doing business in India, meeting etiquette requires a handshake. However, Indians themselves use the *namaste*. This is where the palms are brought together at chest level with a slight bow of the head.

It is advisable to use your right hand while offering something to another person, as the left hand is considered 'unclean'.

In the business world, try not to display anger as this is the worst way to achieve anything in India.

20

4 **Now listen again, stop the recording as necessary, and complete the gaps in the sentences.**

1 I think that India has different ....

2 We have the .... and we also have the wealthy.

3 We have the corporate and we have the ....

4 The corporate is, ... in the world.

5 People have worked very, very hard since .... have come in.

6 Our talent, for a change, is staying in India .... having to look overseas.

7 They felt that their talents .... used.

8 You can still go out and .... with friends.

Clear usage: continuous passive forms

Gayatri says:

'They felt that their talents weren't being used'…. 'They weren't being rewarded enough.'

Compare the continuous passive forms on the left with their active forms on the right:

We are being paid well to do the job.	*They are paying us well to do the job.*
I wasn't being paid very well in my previous job (so I left).	*They weren't paying me very well in my previous job (so I left).*
More business should be being done in Bangladesh. [uncommon use]	*We should be doing more business in Bangladesh.*
The contract will be being signed next week. [uncommon use]	*They will be signing the contract next week.*

Gayatri says that she 'hangs out with friends till midnight'. 'Hanging out' is informal slang meaning to spend time with people, often in a familiar location.

B

David is from Glasgow in Scotland and spends much of his time working with Indian companies. In this recording he gives his impressions on how this work compares with working with companies in the UK and in China.

21

1 Read the comprehension questions below. Then, play the recording through once and answer the questions.

1 How many weeks did David recently spend in India?

2 In his opinion, are there any major differences in the way business is conducted in India compared with China and the UK?

3 What are the main factors which present difficulties and challenges when doing business?

21

2 Now listen again, stop the recording as necessary, and complete the gaps in the sentences.

1 It's quite a .... trip.

2 They're very professional .... of how they're run.

3 Many UK-based people [...], you know, have a .... of how these countries may be.

4 I include myself in that, ... I have a Scottish accent.

5 Most of the companies that we .... with are entirely professional.

6 We're only limited in, sometimes, (the) understanding due to .... differences.

⬚ COBUILD CHECK : attitudes in business

- We can use the **diverse** mix of people to our advantage and share talents.

- The graduate population is questioning the working environment, and with that the management style, **corporate** culture and working hours.

- Sufficient employment **opportunities** is what we need, not legislation outlawing managers with 'ageist' attitudes.

- The company believes in the power of big advertising-led ideas that change consumer **perceptions** and alter their behaviour.

- Throughout his **professional** career, he always believed that it was his duty to use his talents not for his personal gain but for the benefit of society as a whole.

- She said she was particularly **impressed** by the professionalism and dedication of the staff.

- Yesterday's strike was launched after lengthy **negotiations** between management and union officials.

David's business trip

David mentions Delhi, Mumbai, Chennai, Pondicherry and Bangalore. Note where these places are on the map of India.

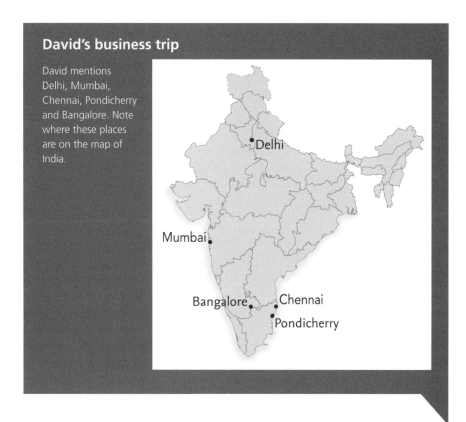

Clear usage: avoiding overcomplicated English

David says:
'Time was spent between many different Indian cities.'

This is a passive sentence. It is sometimes clearer to use the active form when speaking to colleagues whose English is not at a high level. So, if David had been trying to speak clearly and simply, he could have said: *I spent my time visiting many different Indian cities.*

Other examples:

Passive	Active
The day was arranged to include visits to three major suppliers.	*We arranged the day to include visits to three major suppliers.*
They were asked to supply detailed specifications of the machine parts.	*We asked them to supply detailed specifications of the machine parts.*

FURTHER STUDY

For more examples of Scottish and Indian English recordings, go to **www.collinselt.com/businesslistening.**

8 China

A superior man is modest in his speech, but exceeds in his actions.
– Confucius (philosopher)

A

Xianwen is from Wuhan in China and works in the automobile components industry. Here, he makes observations on the way foreign companies deal with Chinese customers and suppliers and makes some suggestions about how to create good relations with Chinese business contacts.

 1 Read the comprehension questions below. Then, play the recording through at least once and answer the questions.

1 In Xianwen's opinion, why do foreign businessmen want to do business with China?

2 In his experience, how are foreign business people treated when they go to China?

3 How has he found that Chinese business people are treated when they go abroad?

4 Why does he think it is important that foreign business people should not come across as being 'arrogant'?

 2 Now listen again. Notice the way that Xianwen pronounces the following words and phrases. Underline any which cause you particular comprehension problems.

– You want to buy something [that] is cheap.

– We just find a car for ourselves and buy the ticket for [our]selves.

– You have to establish a good relationship with the leader.

– So you shouldn't be arrogant. You should be like a friend.

– You shouldn't be the new bird here.

– You should list three or five (of) names.

– You should tell the Chinese businessmen about this.

⊜ COBUILD CHECK : 'relationship'

- Even in jobs not requiring teamwork, **relationships** with co-workers, supervisors or clients can be stressful.

- A good **relationship** was **forged** with local employers before the course commenced by inviting them to a working lunch.

- Credibility comes from being good at what you do, being reliable and trustworthy, and **building** good **relationships**.

- Establishing good **working relationships** can help us secure the cooperation of the people we need to accomplish our tasks.

Chinese proverbs

Xianwen says that foreigners 'should not be the new bird here' meaning that they should not be naïve when coming to China. They should prepare themselves for their visit and in doing so, show respect for their hosts.

Some other Chinese sayings

A drop of water shall be returned with a burst of spring. = Even if you receive just a small favour from someone, you should thank them by returning a bigger favour whenever they need it.

Thirty years the east bank, thirty years the west bank. = Luck and destiny will change over time.

When the tree falls, the monkeys scatter. = When a leader loses power, his followers become disorganised. In English, this is described using the term 'fair weather friends', meaning friends who are only there in the good times.

22

3 **Now listen again, stop the recording as necessary and complete the gaps in the sentences.**

1 You want to establish the [a] factory, because the worker's wage is .... here.

2 ... to 'feel' the culture here, to let you become .... China.

3 You should have a .... plan.

4 You don't want (to) .... to just come by to visit one company.

5 Because they know that they have ....

Clear usage: conditional forms

Xianwen says:

'If you want to come [to] China, if you wanted to have a big contract with us, then your ticket is for us, your hotel fee and your dinner fee is all paid by us.'

In this sentence, 'correct' usage would be to put this sentence into the conditional tense:

If you wanted to come to China, if you wanted to have a big contract with us, then your ticket would be paid for by us, your hotel fee and your dinner fee would all be paid for by us.

Even though Xianwen does not use the 'correct' conditional forms, do you understand what he wants to say?

Some standard conditional forms in English:

If a customer wants to visit our factory in China, we pay all travel costs.

If you come to China, then we will pay for your hotel.

If you were to come to China, we would pay for your hotel.

If you had told us you were coming, we would have made arrangements for you. Don't forget to let us know next time!

B

Ai Lan works for an international sales company in Beijing and is originally from Hong Kong. In this recording, she discusses the importance of establishing a good rapport with Chinese business partners.

1 Read the comprehension questions below. Then, play the recording through once and answer the questions.

1 In what way is doing business in China different from doing business in the western world?

2 In Ai Lan's opinion how should foreign businessmen build a good rapport with their Chinese partners?

3 How should you show your respect for your Chinese partners when having dinner with them?

4 In which area of China does Ai Lan say that this culture is most important?

'Bottoms up' is an informal expression used in English to mean 'cheers'. It came from the idea of turning your glass upside down to pour its entire contents into your mouth, thus turning the *bottom* of the glass *up*wards. However, it no longer means that you should finish your drink "in one gulp"! Now, it's usually just another way of saying 'cheers'.

Ai Lan says: 'a toasting'

'Standard' usage would be: *a toast*

Chinese names

Ai Lan explained a little about her Chinese name: 'My Chinese name is Zhou Ai Lan. In Chinese names, we always put the surname first, whereas with Western names it is the other way round. This is because the family name is important to us. My surname, Zhou, is one of the 10 most common surnames in China. *Ai* means 'love', *lan* means 'orchid flower'. All Chinese names have a meaning, and parents think about these meanings when they give them to their children.'

---

2 Now listen again. Notice the way that Ai Lan pronounces the following words and phrases. Again, underline any words and phrases which you find difficult to understand. Do you find Ai Lan easier to follow than Xianwen? Why? Why not?

– If we know you well, then we can do a lot of things.

– That's why you need to build a relationship or rapport.

– You 'bottoms up' and… it's— you're showing your respect to your partner.

– The more you drink, then the happier you guys are.

– … because then you have the guts to drink with them.

Useful vocabulary and phrases: business socialising

I'd like to propose a toast to Tom Blomqvist. Tom, thank you for all the great work you have done on the project.

What would you like to drink? There is some still and sparkling water and there are some other soft drinks.

It's great to have this opportunity to welcome you here and to show you around our city.

Please accept this gift as a memento of your visit to China.

We have really enjoyed our visit and look forward to welcoming you back in the spring.

Thank you for all your hospitality. Everything has been fantastic.

Some international alternatives to 'Cheers'

À votre santé / Santé (French)
Kippis (Finnish)
Fisehatak / Shucram (Arabic)
Prost (informal) /
Zum Wohl (formal) (German)
Skål (Swedish)
Gan bei (Chinese)
Kampai (Japanese)
Salud (Spanish)
Na zdorovje (Russian)
Chukbae (Korean)

3 Now listen again, stop the recording as necessary and complete the gaps in the sentences.

1 Chinese business .... is very different from [the] Western world.

2 Probably, you know, things will be more ....

3 How do you do that? ...., it's through the social (like) part.

4 Dinner is a good way for you to build the ....

5 It's Chinese ...., not (the) red wine.

6 If you .... a toasting.

Clear usage: stating reasons

Ai Lan says: 'That's why you need to build a relationship.'

Useful phrases for stating your reasons:

The reason for that is you need to build a relationship.
It's vital that you develop rapport.
Unless you build a close relationship, you won't succeed.

Ai Lan says: 'The more you drink, then the happier you guys are.'

Other statements using comparative forms of adjectives:

The less you drink, the better you will feel in the morning.
The harder I work, the less stressed I feel.
The more expensive the final product, the more we can spend on the raw materials.

FURTHER STUDY

For some additional recordings, go to
www.collinselt.com/businesslistening.

9 Making arrangements

If there is a 50-50 chance that something will go wrong, then nine times out of ten it will. – Paul Harvey (American journalist)

A

In the first of three recordings of people making and changing meeting arrangements, Nikki (from Scotland) asks Catrina (from Canada) for some advice.

1 Read the questions and then play the recording through once. Answer the questions to check your understanding of the conversation.

1 Why is Nikki calling?
2 When is Nikki visiting Catrina?
3 What is her 'best option' for getting to the office?
4 How much does the shuttle bus cost?
5 How much would a taxi cost?

2 Now listen again, stop the recording as necessary, and complete the gaps in the sentences.

1 When you arrive, there is .... straight outside.
2 If you need to ...., (that's a) that's a good option.
3 How much do you think that would cost, ...?
4 [It] shouldn't .... more than twenty minutes.
5 So I should have plenty time .... our three o'clock meeting, then.
6 No .... [I'll] look forward to seeing you.

Useful vocabulary and phrases: starting a phone conversation

How (are) you doing? / How are you?

How are things going?

I'm fine / I'm (very) well / I'm good / I'm doing great.

It's great to hear from you.

Do you have five minutes (to talk)?

I'll call back later if this isn't a good time / if now isn't convenient.

Can I call you back this afternoon?

I'm just calling to get some directions.

I just wanted to let you know that I'm still landing at Rio.

I see that we have a meeting in the diary for next Thursday.

Can I just check that you're still OK for Monday? *(colloquial, UK)*

About the meeting next week. What time shall we meet?

Clear usage: question tags

Nikki says:

'OK, but you'd recommend a taxi, would you?'

Note how she uses question tag 'would you?' after the statement 'you'd recommend a taxi'. Native speakers often use question tags when they probably know the answer but nevertheless want to be sure of it. This type of question invites an emphatic (yes/no) response – note Catrina's reply:

'Yes, I'd definitely recommend a taxi.'

Note these other examples of question tags and simple responses:

You're going to Moscow tomorrow, aren't you?	*Yes, I am. On the 3.30 flight.*
You booked the tickets, didn't you?	*Yes, I did. Five days ago.*
You'll call me tomorrow, won't you?	*Yes, I will. I promise.*

Compare with these 'open' questions:

Are you going to Moscow tomorrow?

Did you book the tickets?

Will you call me tomorrow?

B

In this recording, John, who is from southern England, calls Bernardo, who is from Rio de Janeiro in Brazil, to check some arrangements.

 Read the questions and then play the recording through once. Answer these questions to check your overall understanding of the dialogue.

1 Why did John call Bernardo?

2 What is the problem?

3 Why can't Rafael attend the meeting?

4 Which day and time do they fix for the meeting?

⊜ COBUILD CHECK: making plans

- *We recommend that commuters call airlines directly to* **check** *the status of flights.*

- *A lot of the airlines are allowing passengers to* **reschedule** *flights at no extra cost.*

- *There's a flight to London, Heathrow, at ten minutes past ten. You'll have* **plenty of time** *to catch that.*

- *I'm willing to fit it in any time that* **suits** *your schedule.*

- *Businesses can also use the service to set up alerts to their phone for* **calendar** *appointments and incoming emails.*

- *Incidentally, I presume the meeting* **scheduled** *for tomorrow is to deal with the procurement problem?*

Clear usage: referring to future plans

Note these phrases from the recording:

'I'm (I am) still landing at Rio next Thursday.'

John uses the present continuous form of the verb to describe his fixed future plan.

'Friday morning is going to be difficult for me.'

Bernardo uses the 'going to' form of the verb to refer to a previously-arranged future event.

Compare with:

'I'll (I will) see you in Rio.'

Here, Bernardo uses the 'will' form to confirm a future arrangement and to end the conversation.

I'll (I will) call you when I arrive. = I promise to call you when I arrive.

Note that there are many ways of expressing the future in English.

2 **Now listen again. Notice the language that keeps the conversation flowing. Complete the missing words at the beginning of these sentences.**

1 Good, I .... to let you know that I'm still landing at Rio ...

2 I think .... for 2 p.m.?

3 Ah, yeah, I'm ...., actually, 'cos ...

4 My colleague, Rafael, ... be attending the meeting.

5 Would you like to .... any other time?

6 Friday morning is .... difficult for me.

C

In this recording, Grant calls Celia because he needs to change some arrangements. Both speakers are from the south of England.

1 **Read the questions and then play the recording. Answer the questions to check your general understanding of the conversation.**

1 When is the meeting originally scheduled for?

2 Why can't Grant make it at that time?

3 Why can't Celia manage Friday this week?

4 What day and time do they fix for the meeting?

5 Where will the meeting be held?

2 Now listen again, stop the recording as necessary, and complete the gaps in the sentences. The focus here is on some key language for making and changing arrangements.

1 I see that we have a meeting .... for ...

2 I can either .... or we can possibly .... for early the following week.

3 It'll have to be the .... week.

4 Let me just .... for details.

5 Excellent! So, ..., it's next ...

6 Thank you very much for being so ....

Useful vocabulary and phrases: airport arrivals information

Go straight through Arrivals and turn left.

How will I recognise you?

Don't worry, I'll be waiting for you at the barrier with a sign.

Follow the signs to Terminal 3.

Ignore the signs to Baggage Reclaim and go straight to Passport Control.

---

3 The speakers in this recording use a lot of colloquial language. First, read through the phrases, then listen to the recording and check off those that you hear.

It's great to hear from you. ☐   Awesome! ☐

That's fantastic! ☐   Sorry about that. ☐

Brilliant! ☐   When would suit? ☐

No problem. ☐   Does that work for you? ☐

Monday is not great for me. ☐   Is that any good? ☐

Friday's not so good for me,
  I'm afraid. ☐   That would be wonderful. ☐

I'm sorry, but that doesn't
  work for me. ☐

FURTHER STUDY

Listen to the recordings in this unit again and study the transcripts. The speakers are predominantly native speakers of English. Notice the language they use to engage each other. How does this compare with the language you use when making everyday arrangements?

For related material on the subject of 'making arrangements' refer to Unit 4 (Voicemails) and Unit 19 (Meeting and greeting), and visit the accompanying website, **www.collinselt.com/businesslistening.**

10 Business hospitality

More business decisions occur over lunch and dinner than at any other time, yet no MBA courses are given on the subject. – Peter Drucker (Austrian-born American management consultant and author)

A

In this recording, Chisato, from Tokyo in Japan, talks about the best way to develop good relationships with Japanese business partners.

1 Read the questions and then play the recording. Answer the following questions for general comprehension.

1 What, in Chisato's opinion, is the best way to create a good relationship with Japanese people?

2 According to Chisato, what kind of relationship do people have with each other during office hours in Japan?

3 Why is it difficult for 'Western people' to understand the real personalities of Japanese business contacts?

2 Now listen to the recording again. Focus on any particular elements of Chisato's pronunciation which cause you comprehension problems by underlining words and phrases which you find difficult to understand.

- The best way to make a good relationship.
- In that situation, Japanese people show [their] real personality.
- It is [a] very rude attitude.
- It is difficult to understand [the] real personality of the boss.
- We look carefully [at] each other.
- It is important to drink together.

3 Now listen again, stop the recording as necessary, and complete the gaps in the sentences.

1 Our relationship is very ....

2 After that, we go to drink ....

3 We create a good ....

4 ... a new suggestion or .... to do work.

5 Japanese people don't show their .... or real characteristics.

6 Read[ing] the .... is [the] most important thing.

'Nominication'

In this recording, Chisato talks about 'nomination' in Japan. Here are some further guidelines to Japanese drinking culture:

- Do not fill your own glass. You may pour drinks for other members of your party, but do not serve yourself.
- If your boss is present, check that his/her glass is never empty.
- When someone offers to fill your glass, hold it with both hands when they are pouring and then take at least a sip before putting your glass down.

Go to www.collinselt.com/businesslistening to hear more from Chisato as she describes the different stages of what she refers to as a 'Japanese drinking party'. These are, in order, *ichiji kai, niji kai, sanji kai* – literally, 'first party' (probably dinner), 'second party' (drinks), 'third party' (often karaoke).

B

In this next recording, Tonya talks about how her firm, which is based in Atlanta, Georgia, in the US, entertains business clients.

1 Read the questions and then play the recording. Answer the questions to check your overall understanding.

1 How often does Tonya entertain business clients?
2 Where do the partners of her firm take clients?
3 Where does the term 'tailgating' come from?
4 When does 'tailgating' take place?

2 Now listen again, stop the recording as necessary and complete the gaps in the sentences.

1 I will take a ....
2 The partners would have clients or .... in their home.
3 Football games are .... a social event.
4 Where the term came from is, ... a pickup truck.
5 'Tailgating' is actually .... with lots of other people.

⬚ COBUILD CHECK: 'client'

- Many people **entertain clients** in their home, which provides a more personal and comfortable business atmosphere.

- The answer lies in agencies' increasing desperation to **woo** potential new **clients**.

- **Prospective clients** are encouraged to take advantage of an obligation-free consultation.

- He had taken an **overseas client** and two members of his own family for lunch at the restaurant.

- There are a host of other **high-profile clients** who prefer to keep their involvement confidential.

- Our aim is to make **client satisfaction** our first priority.

- He wanted to cultivate **potential clients** and identify gaps in the market.

3 If you are interested in organising a 'tailgate' party, you can find plenty of ideas and recipes on the Internet. Practise some useful language for such a party by putting the words in the box into the correct column. See Unit 11 for food-related discussions in English.

guacamole	hot dogs	baked beans	grill (UK: 'barbecue')
stuffed peppers	chicken legs	potato salad	steak sandwich
olives	silverware	ice	pickles
burgers	relish	drinks	chips (UK: 'crisps')
plates	cooler	ketchup	
salsa	ribs	coleslaw	

Main dishes	Side dishes	Dips/toppings	Food preparation
....	....	....	....
....	....	....	....
....	....	....	....
....	....	....	....
....	....	....	....
....	....	....	....

Clear usage: talking about re-occurring events

Tonya says:

'Occasionally I will take a client out to lunch.'

In this sentence, Tonya uses 'will' in everyday speech to talk about what she does on a regular basis. The use of 'will' can be used to express expected, habitual behaviour – it is not only used to refer to the future. Other examples:

I will (I'll) sometimes spend hours looking for bargain flights.

She will (She'll) always make sure that a job is done well.

In these sentences, the simple present tense can be used as an alternative:

Occasionally, I take a client out to lunch or I occasionally take a client out to dinner.

I sometimes spend hours looking for bargain flights.

She always makes sure that a job is done well.

WARNING: Note that 'tailgating' also means driving too close to the car in front!

Useful vocabulary and phrases: arranging hospitality

Are you free tomorrow evening?

We're having a barbecue.

I hope that you can join us.

What is the dress code?

It's very informal. / It's very casual.

Is there anything that you don't eat?

I'm a vegetarian.

I'm lactose-intolerant.

I have a nut allergy / wheat allergy.

I'll arrange for a car to pick you up at 7 p.m.

See you later!

4 Complete the gaps with words from the box to create popular pastimes around the world. If you could choose to be invited to one of these events, which would it be?

cricket	picnic	karaoke	fondue	~~Formula One~~
skidoo	baseball	shashlik	polo	

e.g. Italy: Watch a ...*Formula One*... race.

1 USA: Go to a .... game.

2 Oman: Eat a .... in the desert.

3 Sweden: Go on a .... safari.

4 Argentina: Be impressed by the skilful horsemanship at a .... tournament.

5 Japan: Entertain colleagues with an evening of ....

6 Kazakhstan: Fill up with a .... barbecue.

7 Switzerland: Share a delicious cheese .... with colleagues.

8 England: Spend a day (or five!) at a .... match.

FURTHER STUDY

Now listen to the recordings in this unit again and study the transcripts. Reflect on times when you have been on the receiving end of business hospitality and have had difficulties in understanding your hosts. For further recordings, including more from Chisato and Tonya, go to **www.collinselt.com/businesslistening.**

11 Talking about food

What is food to one, is to others bitter poison. – Lucretius (Roman philosopher and poet)

A

In this recording, Yue, who is from Beijing in China, recommends one of her favourite dishes.

1 Read the questions and then play the recording. Note down your answers.
1 What dish does Yue particularly recommend?
2 How is it cooked?
3 How do you eat it?
4 What does it taste like?

2 Now listen again. Notice how Yue pronounces the following phrases. Underline any phrases which you found difficult to understand when you first listened to the recording.

- Maybe it's not very healthy.
- The skin of the duck is … crispy.
- Then you can put the meat and skin in the, like, taco thing.
- The sauce is a little sweet.
- It's very delicious.

Talking about food

The English terms used in different regions of the world to refer to food and cooking methods can vary significantly. Here are just a few examples of different food and cooking terms in the US and the UK:

UK	US
barbecue	grill
grill	broil
deep fat fry	fry
fizzy drink/pop	soda
crisps	chips
chips	(French) fries
biscuit	cookie
aubergine	eggplant
gherkin	pickle
courgette	zucchini

COBUILD CHECK: describing food and drink

- *Adding **fizzy** liquids such as soda water or **gassy** beer make wonderful light **crispy** batters.*

- *The mild flavour and **crunchy** texture of Chinese cabbages are good both in salads or a stir-fry.*

- *The ostrich was **chewy**, dark meat that tasted like a cross between pork and beef.*

- *The breakfast menu offers platters of **fluffy** scrambled eggs, and **spicy** sausages.*

- *The end result is delicious – a **sharp** and **tangy** lime sauce accompanied by basmati rice.*

- *This was back in the 1950s, when **overcooked** meat and **soggy** vegetables were our staple diet.*

3 Complete the sentences by circling the correct word.

1 The meat was difficult to eat. It was very [*gristly* / *crunchy*].

2 The beans were the best I have ever had. They were really [*bland* / *tasty*].

3 The steak was so [*chewy* / *tender*], it almost melted in your mouth.

4 Have you ever tried [*poached* / *mashed*] eggs?

5 Do you know any good [*vegetarian* / *vegetable*] restaurants?

6 Venison is a very [*fatty* / *lean*] meat.

7 Did you try [*live* / *living*] octopus when you were in Korea?

8 Bird's nest soup is a [*delicacy* / *delicious*] in China.

B

In this recording, some friends (Japanese, American and Scottish) talk about their experiences of Japanese food.

1 Read the questions. Then play the recording and note down your answers. Do not worry about understanding every word and phrase.

1 What does Saya miss most about Japanese food when she is away from home?

2 According to the speakers, how regularly do Japanese people eat sushi?

3 How does this compare with Nikki's preconceptions about sushi?

4 Where do you go in Japan if you want to buy cheap sushi?

5 What are the components of the set meal recommended by Patrick?

6 What dish does Rie miss most?

2 Now listen to the recording again and complete the gaps in the sentences.

1 What do you .... most?

2 How often do you eat .... in Japan?

3 ... and then a big .... meat and ... then some sushi.

4 Always with the sushi, like some kind of .... or some kind of fish.

5 Well, I think it's bentos, like a ....

6 Or can you .... here?

Before Nikki went to Japan she 'thought that she **would be having** sushi three times a day'. In direct speech this would be:

I expect / think that I'll be having sushi three times a day.

Note that 'will' changes to 'would' in reported speech in standard English. Compare direct speech and reported speech forms in these examples:

Direct speech: *I expect I will (I'll) be eating a lot of raw food.*

Reported speech: *I thought I would be eating a lot of raw food.*

Direct speech: *I will (I'll) arrange it.*

Reported speech: *She said she would arrange it.*

Direct speech: *I eat out two or three times a week.*

Indirect speech: *He told me that he ate out two or three times a week.*

Direct speech: *We've never tried Vietnamese food.*

Indirect speech: *They said that they had never tried Vietnamese food.*

3 **Match the Japanese foods and drink with their definitions. If you have no experience of Japanese food, try using the Internet to find the answers.**

1	tempura	a	Raw fish and seafood
2	sashimi	b	Battered and deep-fried seafood or vegetables
3	gyoza	c	Rice wine
4	bento	d	Chinese-style noodles prepared in a soup
5	ramen	e	A cooking technique where foods are broiled *(US)* / grilled *(UK)* in a soy sauce marinade
6	teriyaki	f	Small savoury, meat-filled fried dumplings
7	sake	g	A packed lunch or a take-away meal in a box consisting of, for example, rice, fish / meat and pickled or cooked vegetables.

C

In this recording, Johny, who is originally from Palestine, talks about his experience of Middle Eastern food in New York.

1 **Read the questions and then play the recording. Check your general comprehension by answering the questions.**

1   What are the two things that Johny missed when he moved to the US?

2   According to Johny, what kind of cooking does not exist in the US?

3   How long did it take him to find the Middle Eastern food he wanted?

2 Play the recording again. Underline any words and phrases in the extracts below to focus on those which you find most difficult to understand.

- Two things when you move to the US.
- You try to find— 'OK, where can I buy some Middle Eastern food?'
- Where can I buy, let's say, hummus?
- Of course, it will take you some time.

3 Match the Middle Eastern specialities with their definitions. If you have no experience of Middle Eastern food, try using the Internet to find the answers. Note that there are many versions of these dishes in different countries – and many spellings!

shawarma	hummus	pitta bread	baba ghanoush
tabouleh	falafel	baklava	kibbeh

1 A meatball dish made with lamb or beef, cracked wheat and pine nuts. ....

2 Mashed aubergine (eggplant) which is mixed with various seasonings depending on the country/region where it is prepared. It is often eaten as a dip. ....

3 A sandwich-like wrap stuffed with grilled meat (for example lamb, goat, chicken, beef). The meat is usually grilled on a revolving spit. ....

4 A chickpea dip. The chickpeas are mashed together with tahini, olive oil, garlic and lemon juice. It is served with pitta bread. ....

5 Fried balls which are made of chickpeas, onions and spices. ....

6 A sweet dessert consisting of layers of filo pastry, syrup and nuts. ....

7 A salad made with cracked wheat, mint, parsley and some other ingredients. ....

8 It can be toasted, stuffed, or dipped in dishes such as baba ghanoush. Served with almost every meal. ....

FURTHER STUDY

When do you need to understand English menus and to talk about food and drink in English? Check the words and phrases in English that you need in a good bilingual dictionary. Research podcasts on the web related to your favourite foods. Listen to the recordings in this unit again and study the transcripts.

For further recordings, including more from Johny and a description of eating out in Korea, go to **www.collinselt.com/businesslistening.**

12 Work-life balance

My beliefs are that the business needs to serve the family rather than the family serve the business. – Kathy Ireland (American entrepreneur)

A

In this recording, Nick, who is from the south of England, talks about how he tries to maintain a good work-life balance.

1 Read the questions and then play the recording through once. Answer the questions for general comprehension.

1 Why was it easy for Nick to commute into London when he was working in Cork Street?
2 Did he enjoy commuting to work by train from the Sussex countryside?
3 Why is he prepared to put up with his long everyday commute to work?
4 How old are his children now?
5 How far does Nick live from the south coast of the UK?

2 Now listen again, stop the recording as necessary, and complete the gaps in the sentences.

1 It was in the days before they put .... all over the south east of London.
2 I wasn't living .... then.
3 The idea .... the train from there is a bit of a pain.
4 I've got to get .... to Hammersmith.
5 I can .... phone call or two.
6 The commuting is just something I have to .... because I don't like living in town.
7 So, I put up with the .... of the day-to-day commute to have nice times in the evenings.
8 It was .... when the kids were younger.
9 … twelve to thirteen hours when you are away from the house is always gonna be ....
10 I'll sacrifice the .... for that.

Useful vocabulary and phrases: some idiomatic phrases used by Nick

to jump on the tube = to go by underground/subway/metro

to put up with something = to tolerate something

the hassle = irritation, annoyance

the telly = the television

it's kind of swapped around = the situation has reversed

the daily grind = the daily (tedious/boring) routine

London

Nick mentions a variety of towns, regions and stations in and around his home town of London, some of which are better known than others. Here is a list of the places he mentions.

Cork Street is in the 'West End' of London – close to the city centre.

Clapham – a (mostly residential) area of south London. Clapham Junction is a major railway station used by commuters.

Purley and **Coulsdon** are 'commuter towns' in the county of Surrey, approximately 30 minutes by train from London.

Victoria is a major railway station and also the site of the main London coach station.

The best-known town in **the county of Sussex** is probably the seaside town of Brighton.

Hammersmith and **Streatham** are boroughs (areas) in west London.

3 Match the words and phrases 1–6 taken from the recording with words and phrases a–f which have similar meanings.

1	jump on	a	travel back and forth (to work)
2	put up with	b	bother
3	commute	c	catch
4	hassle	d	relocate
5	swap	e	tolerate
6	move out	f	change round

32

4 Notice that Nick uses a variety of phrases that give him time to think as he speaks. Play the recording again and listen out for the following. Tick them when you hear them. (He doesn't use them all!)

Sort of …	☐	I just …	☐
A bit of a …	☐	I think that's …	☐
The idea of …	☐	You know, …	☐
But hey …	☐	It's kind of …	☐
So …	☐	As I say, …	☐

⪪ COBUILD CHECK: the daily commute

- *Taking the daily **commute** out of work could greatly enhance the quality of people's lives.*

- *Research confirms that people who regularly **commute** long distances to and from work are unhappier than those who work closer to home.*

- *The storm slowed rush-hour **traffic** to a five-mile-an-hour crawl.*

- *For many of us a car is a quick and relatively cheap way of getting from A to B without the **hassles** of public transport.*

- *I don't have to commute, as my daily **journey** to work involves walking up one flight of stairs to my study.*

- *London Underground police announced that passengers on **the tube** would be randomly stopped and their bags searched.*

Nick uses the present continuous form of the verb even though he is describing his regular routine:

'You're leaving at six-thirty in the morning.'

'You're getting back at seven o'clock at night.'

The simple present tense is more often used to talk about routines:

> *I usually leave for work at 6.30 a.m.*

> *I often don't get home till 7 p.m.*

However, Nick wants to emphasise what is clearly sometimes a tedious routine and this sentiment is well expressed by using the present continuous form. Native speakers often use the continuous form of the present tense to express irritation, e.g.:

> *Why am I always having to wait for you?* = Why do I always have to wait for you?

> *Why is it always raining at the weekend?* = Why does it always rain at the weekend?

The present continuous is also used by speakers on mobile phones to describe what is happening right now:

> *Where are you? I'm just walking to the station.*

> *Are you still at the hotel? Yes – still waiting for the taxi.*

B

Tonya is from Atlanta, Georgia, in the USA. In this recording, she talks about the work ethic of the 'next generation'.

1 **Read the questions and then play the recording through once. Answer the questions to check your general understanding of what she says.**

1 According to Tonya, is the 'next generation' prepared to work up to sixty hours a week when required?

2 Does she think that the United States has a strong work ethic in general?

3 What does Tonya consider to be the negative side of a very strong work ethic?

> Tonya says that 'a strong work ethic is to our demise at times' – 'demise' means 'death' or 'end' so this is a rather strong statement!

COBUILD CHECK: work-life balance

- *Senior managers stipulated **work-life balance** as their main criterion when choosing jobs.*

- *Low-skilled labour and a declining **work ethic** are posing a threat to business activity.*

- ***Burnout** can happen in professions like training where it seems as if you are giving all the time and never receiving.*

- *I was married for 14 years before **work pressure** wrecked my marriage, and we divorced.*

- *More than a third of absences were due to **stress-related** illnesses.*

- *He was quite tired of the dreary **daily commute** to work and, frankly, his job didn't excite him any longer.*

2 Now listen again, stop the recording as necessary, and complete the gaps in the following paragraph.

I understand and **1** .... that the next generation coming through is **2** .... to contribute up to sixty hours a week during busy season. As a culture, I think the United States has a very **3** .... in general. Obviously not everyone, but in general. I also think that strong work ethic is to **4** .... at times. It certainly doesn't contribute to the family unit **5** .... to be working sixty hours a week and never be home for dinner for three months out of the year. That's not good for us. So I think it's a **6** ...., I do.

3 Underline the adjectives below which refer to people with a strong work ethic. There are one or two in each line. Check the meaning of any unfamiliar words in the Mini-dictionary at the back of the book. Which of these qualities would you use to refer to your work ethic and which to that of your colleagues?

1 determined	lazy	motivated
2 unmotivated	negative	ambitious
3 strong-minded	idle	lethargic
4 positive	decisive	indecisive
5 reluctant	hesitant	keen
6 tenacious	persistent	sluggish

FURTHER STUDY

Now listen to the recordings in this unit again and study the transcripts. Reflect on the comments made by Nick and Tonya in relation to your own work-life balance. For further recordings of Nick and Tonya, go to **www.collinselt.com/businesslistening**

13 Talking about your work

Work is the refuge of people who have nothing better to do. – Oscar Wilde
(Irish writer and poet)

A

Gosia is from Wroclaw in Poland and works in the Facilities department of a large international business. In this recording she talks about her work conducting inductions for new employees into her company.

1 Read the comprehension questions below. Then, play the recording through once and answer the questions.

1 How often does Gosia conduct the induction for new employees?
2 Which inductions precede the Facilities induction?
3 How does she conduct the induction?
4 What is the first place that she points out to new employees?
5 What does she tell them about the canteen?

2 Read the following phrases aloud and then listen out for them as you play the recording. Compare your pronunciation with Gosia's.

– I'm responsible for the induction.
– We've got a few people down in Facilities, and we do share inductions.
– We usually get a list of new employees sent by HR.
– We talk about fire issues, health and safety stuff …
– I explain [the] structure of the building.

Useful office vocabulary

fire exit	post room *(UK)* / mail room *(US)*
fire alarms	reception / lobby
fire extinguishers	corridor
swing / revolving doors	canteen *(UK)* / cafeteria *(US)*
conference room	canteen / cafeteria manager
lift *(UK)* / elevator *(US)*	first aider
staircase	security guard
escalator	receptionist
toilets *(UK)* / restrooms *(US)*	maintenance staff
kitchen / kitchenette	fire warden
HR (Human Resources) / Personnel	garage / parking

Clear usage: 'the' (the definite article)

Note that Gosia sometimes leaves out the definite article 'the':

'I meet them in [the] HR office'
'I explain [the] structure of the building'
'I take them down to [the] canteen'

Many non-native speakers of English omit the article as their languages do not follow English patterns of article usage. Gosia and other Polish speakers of English are not alone.

34

3 **Now listen again, stop the recording as necessary, and complete the gaps in the sentences.**

1 We know how many people are ....
2 I .... in the HR office.
3 Part of the induction is (like) a walk through the ....
4 ... where they can find the .... lift, a toilet, etc.
5 I take them down to [the] ...., explain what they can expect.
6 And then walk through the .... room.

4 **Match the words on the left with those on the right which have similar meanings.**

1	induction	a	personnel
2	HR	b	lobby
3	lift	c	orientation
4	corridor	d	restrooms
5	toilets	e	passage
6	reception	f	elevator
7	garage	g	exit
8	way out	h	parking

⊜ COBUILD CHECK: the work environment

- *An on-site **facilities manager** attends to security, cleaning and upkeep issues.*

- *This is an area which should be covered by regulations on **health and safety** at work.*

- *The key to successful **induction** is enabling the new employee to be confident in the new situation.*

- *Have all staff members participate in a video **orientation** when they start their jobs, and, if necessary, make it available in languages other than English.*

- *Increased holiday entitlement, a subsidized **canteen**, free or cut-price products, or private health care insurance, are examples of such non-financial rewards.*

B

Taressa is from Brisbane, the capital of Queensland, Australia.
In this recording she talks about her first job.

35

1 Read the statements below. Then, play the recording through once and decide whether they are true or false.

		True	False
1	Taressa studied Politics and Journalism at university.		
2	Her first job was as an advisor to a Government minister.		
3	The day-to-day job was quite dull.		
4	She felt that the job was perfect for a long-term career.		
5	The job helped her to develop her problem-solving and thinking processes.		

Clear usage: 'have' and 'get'

Have and *get* are often used in informal speech in English. Note the expressions that Taressa uses in the recording.

have/had
'It had my blood pumping every single day.'

get/got
'I got involved in a political party.'
'You get put under a lot of pressure.'
'I'm beginning to get the feel for what I have to do in this job.'

35

2 Now listen again, stop the recording as necessary, and complete the gaps in the sentences.

1 I .... with a political party.

2 ... through my involvement, ... myself a fantastic job.

3 It was something that, you know, had my .... every single day.

4 There's always some sort of ...., always ....

5 There is quite a high .... rate.

6 You sort of had to not have that many .... or .... expectations of yourself.

7 You always have to .... up.

8 It's given me a great work ....

Useful vocabulary and phrases: talking about a past job

I've always been interested in …

My first job involved organising / running …

It gave me a lot of valuable experience.

The most exciting thing about the job was …

After a few years I decided to move on.

I realised that I needed to have some new challenges.

I was promoted in 2011.

I was responsible for …

It was a great job.

3 **Continue the sentence which starts in the left hand column with a phrase from the right hand column.**

1	I've always been interested …	a	brilliant job.
2	I landed myself a …	b	long-term.
3	I got fed up with all …	c	in politics.
4	You have to be prepared to …	d	affairs.
5	People think that the job is …	e	the back-stabbing.
6	You have to have a certain …	f	glamorous.
7	It's not something I want to do …	g	roll your sleeves up.
8	There were always …	h	work ethic.

⬡ COBUILD CHECK: office politics

- Those in power still love the sound of their own voices and the **backstabbing** still continues, although today they tend to use the media rather than a knife.

- He was being **groomed** for the job but was so fed up with the management attitudes that he went overseas and did not come back.

- We all have two choices in this situation – either walk away or **roll your sleeves up** and tackle the problem head on.

- It's a tall order to ask someone to do hard **yakka*** in dangerous, wet, uncomfortable conditions for hours on end for no pay. (Australian)

- A fundamental, unwritten rule of **office politics** is getting what you want is easier when you give others what they want.

*hard yakka = (Australian slang) hard work

FURTHER STUDY

For further recordings, including more from Gosia and Taressa, go to **www.collinselt.com/businesslistening.**

14 Finance and accounting

Most of the successful people I've known are the ones who do more listening than talking. – Bernard Baruch (American financier)

A

Liz is from Tauranga in New Zealand and works as a management accountant. In this first recording she talks about her current studies and about the role of management and financial accountants.

 1 Read the comprehension questions below. Then, play the recording through once and answer the questions.

1 What does CIMA stand for?

2 Which areas do financial accountants focus on?

3 How does their work compare with management accountants?

 2 Listen again. Notice the way that Liz pronounces the following words and phrases. Compare your pronunciation of these words with hers. Notice, for example, how Liz pronounces management ('manidjment') as 'minidgment'.

– I'm studying for CIMA.

– They would be more focused on balance sheets and P&Ls.

– There are strict guidelines.

– A management accountant normally is more internally focused.

– … how to get the best out of things.

 3 Now listen again, stop the recording as necessary, and complete the gaps in the sentences.

1 … a global body that looks after CIMA-………………………………… accountants.

2 There's also ACA and ACCA, and they are ………………………………… accountants.

3 That's what you would have to be to be an ………………………………… .

4 If you were presenting accounts to ………………………………… .

5 … management within a ………………………………… .

6 … to get the best ………………………………… that you can have …

7 … while operating the business ………………………………… presenting stuff externally.

⊑ COBUILD CHECK: the world of finance

- The acquisition is subject to financing and approvals by regulators and **shareholders**.

- The truth is management today must balance the concerns of many groups of **stakeholders**.

- **Stockholders** are one group; others include customers, employees, vendors, ultimate consumers.

- Under current rules, the **accrued** interest is deductible by the company issuing the debt.

- The basic books of account are divided into **ledgers** – sales ledger, purchases ledger – the name derives from the days when separate books were kept for each.

- We plan to severely cut back our overheads, so that our **cash flow** is positive.

---

4 Choose words from the box to complete the sentences.

assets	shareholder	currencies
cash flow	interest	ledgers

1 Business accounts transactions are recorded in the ....

2 The company is having .... problems. Too much money is going out and not enough is coming in.

3 Being a .... in a company going through a financial crisis is not easy!

4 We are considering selling some of our .... to raise some cash for the business.

5 We hold bank accounts in a number of major ....

6 .... rates have been very low recently so we have been able to borrow money and make some major investments.

B

In this second part of the recording, Liz talks about the wider financial organisation in her company.

1 Read the comprehension questions below. Then, play the recording through once and answer the questions.

1 Is the separate Finance Division based in the same place as Liz's team?

2 What is the nitty-gritty job that she refers to?

3 Does the Finance Director focus just on the management accountancy part of the business?

Only use acronyms and abbreviations without explanation when talking to colleagues who also use and understand them. Liz uses the following acronyms:

> *CIMA = Chartered Institute of Management Accountancy – the world's largest professional body of management accountants.*
>
> *ACCA = Association of Chartered Certified Accountants – global*
>
> *ACA = Association of Consulting Actuaries – UK-based*
>
> *P&L = profit and loss (account)*
>
> *CEO = Chief Executive Officer*
>
> *FD = Finance Director*

37

2 **Play the recording again and pause it as necessary as you complete the key vocabulary gaps in the sentences.**

1 I work within the management accountancy ....

2 There's a separate .... within our company that looks after the .... ledger.

3 ... talking about what's sitting on our .... sheet ...

4 ... how our .... is coming together.

5 They look after the ....

6 He will be looking after the people that are .... currency.

Clear usage: 'will' and 'would'

Liz says:

'Our FD would be looking after ...'

'He will be looking after such a broad range.'

'Once you're that senior you would be doing a whole lot of accounts stuff.'

Note that in these examples, *will* does not mean 'future' and *would* does not mean 'conditional'. Liz is using these continuous modal forms to describe the everyday work of the Finance Director.

Compare with the more everyday use of these structures:

> *I will be working on the report tomorrow.*
>
> *I would be working on the report tomorrow, but unfortunately I haven't received all the data I need.*

C

Tonya is from Atlanta, Georgia, in the United States. In this recording, she talks briefly about her job as an accountant.

38

1 Read the statements below. Then, play the recording through once and decide whether they are true or false.

	True	False
1 Her company employs one hundred people.		
2 She reviews financial statements and ensures her department complies with accounting standards.		
3 She has just left her previous job in a Fortune 500 company.		
4 She has worked as an external and an internal auditor.		

38

2 Listen again, pause the recording as necessary, and complete the key vocabulary gaps in the sentences.

1 I am a CPA in .... practice.

2 I work with a small accounting ....

3 My day-to-day activities as an accountant involve .... financial statements ...

4 ...and .... that my department is .... with the applicable accounting standards.

5 I do a .... of research.

6 I also do some .... for our firm.

7 .... to that I worked with a large, publicly-traded Fortune 500 company.

8 My role there was as an .... auditor.

Useful vocabulary and phrases: accountancy

Tonya is a **CPA**, which stands for a Certified Public Accountant. This is a statutory title which is given to qualified accountants in the United States who have passed the 'Uniform Certified Public Accountant Examination'.

The **Fortune 500** is a list which ranks the top 500 US publicly and privately-held companies. It is compiled and published by *Fortune* magazine. It was first published in 1955.

An **internal auditor** is an employee of a company who examines company accounts to ensure no fraud is being committed and to make sure that board directives and management policies are correctly executed.

An **external auditor** is an independent accountant, not employed by the company, who examines company accounts.

FURTHER STUDY

There are many examples of recordings dealing with financial matters on websites such as ft.com, reuters.com and the financial websites of many newspapers. If this is an area where you need listening practice, there is a wide variety of resources to draw from.

You can also listen to further recordings of Liz and Tonya if you go to **www.collinselt.com/businesslistening.**

15 Parental leave and redundancy

You have a lifetime to work, but children are only young once.
– Polish proverb

A

In the first recording in this unit, Catherine, who is from the south of England, talks about the laws concerning maternity and paternity leave in the UK.

1 Read the comprehension questions below. Then, play the recording through once and answer the questions.

1 According to Catherine, for how long must your job be left open for you to be able to resume work after you have taken maternity leave?

2 What percentage of your salary do you receive during the first 6 weeks of maternity leave?

3 Do you have the right to get your original job back when you return?

4 What do most companies offer their staff in terms of paternity leave?

5 In Catherine's experience, how much time off work do most fathers take?

2 Read through the phrases below and then listen to the recording again. Note how Catherine pronounces the phrases in 'RP' English. Do you find Catherine easy to understand?

– You have the right to keep your job open.
– The statutory maternity leave is something like six weeks …
– I think you're allowed that for the following nine months or so.
– If you take the full twelve months, there is a financial sacrifice.
– You do have the right to go back to your original job or an equivalent job.
– Most companies just give you two weeks' extra holiday.
– It doesn't have to be at the birth of the baby.
– Most people I know take the two weeks.
– They end up taking three weeks or a month off work if they can.

Useful vocabulary and phrases: away on leave

Who is covering for Fiona while she is away on leave?
Teresa is covering for / standing in for her.
When is she due back to work?

When is the baby due?
When is she due to leave hospital?
Please pass on our best wishes.

⊜ COBUILD CHECK: maternity and paternity leave

- *The provision of **maternity leave** benefits has helped to establish good rapport with employees.*

- *Sweden and France offer the most generous **parental leave** programs, and while these programs are expensive, they're considered essential.*

- *HP appreciates the 'personal' life needs of an employee. Beyond providing **statutory leave**, an additional leave of 10 days is provided for employees who are getting married.*

- ***Paternity leave** should be paid at 90% of earnings, and mothers should be entitled to transfer to partners some or all of the second six months of their year's maternity leave entitlement.*

- *The trend toward working later in **pregnancy** and coming back faster produced a consistent drop in time lost to pregnancy.*

- *They recognise the **financial sacrifice** made by mothers or fathers who stay at home full-time to look after children.*

3 Use the vocabulary in the box to complete the gaps in the sentences.

cover	disruption	birth	entitled
sacrifice	due	statutory	notice

1 You're pregnant? That's great news! When is the baby ....?

2 Who's going to .... for you while you're on maternity leave?

3 Two members of staff were on parental leave out of a team of five, and the company did not arrange cover so inevitably there was a lot of ....

4 I was .... to take four weeks' leave, but I only took two weeks.

5 I took 12 months' maternity leave, but the financial .... was worth it.

6 My colleague had some problems with HR as she didn't give sufficient prior .... of when she expected to have the baby.

7 Conditions concerning .... maternity leave differ from country to country.

8 Were you present at your baby's ....?

Clear usage: passive and active forms

Catherine says: 'Your job has to be kept open for you for 12 months.'

Note the use of the passive form 'has to be kept open'. The passive form tends to be used in fairly formal statements. Here are some examples:

Passive forms	**Active alternatives**
Prior notice has to be given.	*You have to give prior notice.*
All employees have to be informed.	*You have to inform all employees.*
Arrangements have to be made.	*You have to make all the arrangements.*

B

In the next recording, David, who is from Glasgow in Scotland, talks about the paternity leave that he took when his children were born.

 1 Read the comprehension questions below. Then, play the recording through once and answer the questions. How do you feel about David's attitudes to parental leave?

1 How old are David's children now?

2 How much time did David take off when his wife had a baby?

3 Does he believe that men should have the same entitlement to parental leave as women?

4 Would he have made different domestic arrangements if he had had more parental leave?

 2 Play the recording again and notice how David pronounces the following phrases. Note in particular his pronunciation of the words in bold.

– My wife who, at that **time, worked** for the same company …

– It is an improvement in the system that men do **gain** paternity **rights**.

– Looking after the children kind of longer **term**.

– It may suit some **families better**.

– We had already arranged for my **wife** to come back to work.

 3 Now play the recording again, pause it where necessary, and fill in the gaps in these sentences.

1 Fathers .... the same paternity rights as they are currently.

2 The rest of the time I took off as .... leave.

3 I don't think they should get .... as the mother.

4 In my ...., it wouldn't have affected me.

5 We'd lined up .... childcare.

6 That had always been .... when we were arranging to plan a family.

C

In this recording, Catherine talks about how she was made redundant from her job whilst on maternity leave and how she set about finding a new job.

 1 Read the comprehension questions below. Then, play the recording through once and answer the questions.

1 Did being made redundant come as a total surprise to Catherine?

2 Who called her?

3 What reason was she given for being made redundant?

4 How did she get her first job after being made redundant?

5 How did she get the job she is doing now?

☰ COBUILD CHECK: 'redundancy'

- *The shutdown was cushioned by **redundancy payments**, retraining and a buoyant labour market.*

- *Thousands of bank employees **face redundancy** as their employers cut costs.*

- *In Britain, when a worker is **'made redundant'** the government picks up part of the check. (US)*

- *Factory officials estimate that more than 10% of*

*the work force here is **redundant**, but layoffs aren't allowed. (US) – ('redundant', in this US example, means having nothing to do)*

- *The company said the 160 employees at the Utah center will receive **severance pay** and assistance in finding new jobs. (US)*

- *Officials told him of their vague dissatisfaction, but he received neither dismissal warnings nor an opportunity to improve before **he was fired**.*

 2 **Play the recording again, pause it where necessary, and complete the gaps in the following sentences.**

41

1 I was .... last year and it was a bit of a shock.

2 I .... to be on maternity leave at the time.

3 I had told the company that I .... going back to work.

4 I got a phone call at home from my .... who wasn't based in the UK.

5 ... after the initial conversation that the whole thing ....

6 I .... with some people I hadn't got in touch with for years.

7 I got the .... almost immediately.

8 ... and I .... for the role I'm currently in.

Useful vocabulary and phrases: being sympathetic

I was very sorry to hear you lost your job.

How is the job search going?

Have you found a new job yet?

Have you tried the ... agency?

Good luck with the interview.

How did the interview go?

Clear usage: talking about past experiences

Catherine says: 'It wasn't a total surprise, given some of the things that had been happening in the company.'

Note how Catherine contrasts her past experiences by using the simple past tense ('It wasn't a surprise') and the continuous form of the past perfect ('things had been happening'). Using this form of the verb indicates that the events had been continuing for some time before Catherine lost her job.

Compare:

They **had already fired** two other employees.

They **had been offering** early retirement to their staff for the last two years.

FURTHER STUDY

If you would like to listen to more further recordings, including an American view on maternity leave, go to **www.collinselt.com/businesslistening**.

16 Planning a business trip

I travel not to go anywhere, but to go. I travel for travel's sake. The great affair is to move. – Robert Louis Stevenson (Scottish novelist and poet)

A

In this recording, David, who is from Glasgow in Scotland, talks about the practicalities of planning a business trip to India.

1 Read the comprehension questions below. Then, play the recording through once and answer the questions.

1 What does David think the success of a business trip depends on?
2 What were the key purposes of the preparatory work for the trip?
3 What was David's PA's role in planning the visit?
4 What was the reason for one of the supplier visits going wrong?
5 Why couldn't David get through to the suppliers by phone?
6 Where were the suppliers' premises located?

COBUILD CHECK: sporting language

David says: 'Meetings were **teed up** over the course of four weeks.' This saying comes from golf, where you tee up your ball before hitting it.

Some other sayings based on sports:

- In January ABB **kicked off** what it claims is the biggest-ever outsourced-maintenance agreement in the pulp-and-paper industry. (football/soccer)

- The idea that boards can pick and choose the type of shareholder they want is one that should be **kicked into touch**. (rugby)

- To provide some insight into how he makes big deals fast, he agreed to provide a **blow-by-blow** account of his biggest acquisition to date. (boxing)

- He was convinced the deal would be an easy victory – 'a **slam dunk**,' in Wall Street parlance. (basketball)

- I would look at existing brands as banging out singles and doubles, and research and development as an area that would hit some **home runs**. (baseball)

- He was always **moving the goalposts** so that we could never anticipate what he wanted. (football / soccer)

- Negotiators again worked right **down to the wire** to reach an agreement. (horse racing)

2 Now listen again, stop the recording as necessary, and complete the gaps in the sentences.

1 Meetings were .... up over the course of four weeks.
2 ... the way in which you can assess the abilities of .... suppliers.
3 I had .... created by my Product Support Manager.

4 He('s) .... together all of the necessary data.

5 Of the .... of meetings which were attended.

6 They had actually recently moved ....

7 It was all .... because we were in the wrong place at the right time.

8 It .... they were two hours outside the city.

9 We have to .... the appointment for another time.

Clear usage: direct questions

David says:

'They eventually called us to say: Are you coming for your meeting?'

This type of language is more direct than saying: *They called to ask us if we were still coming to the meeting.*

Other examples:

   And then he said to me: What are you doing there?
   I wanted to ask him: Who is going to make all the transport arrangements?

David also talks clearly about actions which **had taken place** before the visit:
   'The suppliers **had** actually **moved** premises.'
   'All the instructions they **had provided** were irrelevant.'

See also 'Clear usage' on page 63.

---

3 Complete the sentences using words from the box. In some cases, more than one of the options is possible.

prepare	coordinate	reschedule	assist
pull together	line up	turn out	attend

1 There was an airline strike so we had to .... the meeting.

2 It was a difficult job to .... all of the parties involved in the project.

3 Is everyone going to be able to .... the meeting?

4 I'm afraid that things didn't .... as we had expected.

5 We have asked our agents to .... meetings with prospective suppliers in the area.

6 My assistant has managed to .... all of the information we need to proceed.

7 I managed to .... what I thought was a great presentation.

8 I'd be very grateful if you could .... me in planning the itinerary for my visit.

4 Match each verb on the left with the one on the right with the most similar meaning.

1	sort out	**a**	plan
2	schedule	**b**	cancel
3	postpone	**c**	fix
4	back out	**d**	arrive
5	delegate	**e**	reduce
6	cut down	**f**	hand over
7	co-ordinate	**g**	defer
8	turn up	**h**	synchronise

B

In this recording, Jude, who is from the south of England, talks about the issues she had to consider when making trips to the Middle East.

1 Read the comprehension questions below. Then, play the recording once and answer the questions.

1 What is the working week in the Middle East?
2 What does Jude say she had to be aware of in her everyday work?
3 How long did she usually spend in the UAE?
4 What was her longest trip to the Middle East?

Greetings and festivals in the Middle East

The traditional Islamic greeting is *Asalamu alaykum* (Peace be with you). If you use this greeting, you will receive the reply *Wa alaykum salam* (And peace be with you).

You should avoid doing business in the Middle East during the month of Ramadan. During this period, Muslims will fast from dawn until dusk, and in many organisations, business activities will be reduced drastically.

It is also advisable to avoid trying to do business during the two important Eid festivals: *Eid al-Fitr*, which follows Ramadan and *Eid al-Adha* which follows the annual pilgrimage to Mecca.

2 Now listen again, stop the recording as necessary, and complete the gaps in the sentences.

1 Not least because you're .... with a different culture.
2 And you have to take into .... stuff like ...
3 I had to time my trips ....
4 It's just being aware of cultural ....
5 ... and making sure that you .... yourself within that context.
6 Sometimes I'd try and .... a couple of territories.
7 ... and then .... to Beirut afterwards.

ⒺCOBUILD CHECK: cultural sensitivities

- To cater for **cultural sensitivities**, the house had gender-segregated bathrooms, bedrooms, sitting areas and prayer rooms.

- They plan to provide information to make Australian business people more **aware** of Indonesia's business culture and commercial environment.

- A manufacturer has to be **sensitive** to local language and idiosyncrasies.

- It can be extremely difficult for an adult to **adapt** psychologically to a culture that is different from the one for which their family of origin prepared them.

- I told them that if their actions are not **respectful** of local customs, then problems may develop.

Clear usage: use of 'would' instead of 'used to'

Note that Jude says:

'I'd be based in London throughout.'

'I'd try and tag on a couple of territories.'

'That would generally take me about 10 days.'

As alternatives, Jude could have said:

I used to be based in London.

I used to try and tag on a couple of territories.

That generally used to take me about 10 days.

Note how Jude contracts the full form *I would* to *I'd*. This is common for native speakers and can cause problems for listeners.

> Note Jude's use of some colloquial British English terms which would not be universally understood:
>
> 'to tag on' = *to add*
>
> 'to nip to' = *to make a quick visit to*

FURTHER STUDY

For some additional recordings, including more from Jude and David, go to **www.collinselt.com/businesslistening.**

17 Cross-cultural negotiation

Men build too many walls and not enough bridges. – Isaac Newton
(English physicist, mathematician and philosopher)

A

In this recording, Chisato, from Tokyo in Japan, discusses her experiences of negotiating with people from European countries.

1 Read the questions and then play the recording. Answer the questions to your general understanding of what Chisato says.

1 What kind of behaviour does Chisato describe as being 'rude'?

2 In Chisato's opinion, Confucianism encourages people to do what?

3 How does a Japanese boss feel when Western business partners insist that their opinion is the right one?

2 Now listen again. Underline any words or phrases which you find difficult to understand because of Chisato's pronunciation. Note in particular her pronunciation of the 'r' in words like 'rude'.

1 … a very rude attitude

2 they suggest another solution

3 Mainly, the boss is much older than the businessman.

4 It is good for business but it is bad for [the] relationship.

5 It is difficult to adjust.

3 Rewrite Chisato's sentences below in 'standard' English.

e.g. Japanese people think insist their opinion is a very rude attitude for colleague.

Japanese people think that it is rude to insist that your opinion is right.

1 The boss order some works for Western country people.

....

2 Mainly the boss is much older.

....

3 Sometimes Western people insist their opinion.

....

4 So it is difficult to adjust Western people, I guess.

....

COBUILD CHECK: playing by the rules

- *Employers are also fully empowered to dismiss employees who refuse to **obey** safety rules.*

- *Failing to **comply with** regulations can cost an organisation thousands if not millions of dollars in fines.*

- *She does not have to **conform to** media or peer pressure in order to be accepted.*

- *They will discipline people who are not **abiding by** the rules of the organisation, or fulfilling their contract.*

- *The company had **contravened** market regulations by offering incentives to travel agencies to boost the sale of tickets for its flights.*

- *Private companies protect themselves by **flouting** the market rules that are supposed to guarantee efficiency.*

- *If I **go against** the desires of the electorate I risk being voted out at the next election.*

- *Both groups **insisted on** the crucial importance of continuous advertising in good times and bad.*

B

In this recording, Frederic, who is from Brittany in the west of France, discusses a different style of negotiating.

 1 Read the questions and then play the recording. Are these statements true or false?

	True	False
1 In France, people like to make quick decisions with little argument or discussion.		
2 He acknowledges that the French way of negotiating can be perceived as rude by Japanese and Chinese people.		
3 He believes that asking lots of questions in business negotiations is a positive thing.		

 2 Now listen again, stop the recording as necessary, and complete the gaps in these sentences.

1 I would describe the way business .... in France as quite dynamic.

2 ... before .... decision to challenge a little bit [the] opinions of people.

3 It could be sometimes .... as a bit .... or a bit rude.

4 It is something that you need to understand and to expect as something positive .... something negative.

 3 Frederic is a clear and fluent speaker of English but he makes some minor 'mistakes'. Do these mistakes cause you to misunderstand what he says? Rewrite these sentences in 'standard' English.

1 People that like to argument ...

....

2 If somebody care of what you're doing …

………

3 If someone care of your opinion …

………

4 He will probably challenge you and ask you a lot of question.

………

ⒸⒺ COBUILD CHECK: attitudes towards different negotiating styles

- If the approach of the law were overly **intrusive**, legitimate entrepreneurial activity might be discouraged.

- He has an uncanny knack of making crass, **insensitive** remarks that offend people.

- She stepped down from her PR firm after making **indiscreet** remarks to a newspaper reporter.

- It was true he had a volatile temperament; he could be **tactless**, hot-tempered and downright **rude**.

- The agents went out of their way to conduct business in a professional and **courteous** manner.

- This type of approach only serves to reinforce the **perception** that IT professionals are not good at people skills.

- She is a most **perceptive** interviewer, who actually listens to the answers to her questions.

---

4 Note how Frederic describes how business is conducted in France. He uses adjectives that suggest positive and negative attributes.

'I would describe the way business is conducted in France as quite *dynamic*.'

'It could be sometimes perceived as a bit *intrusive*.'

Which of the following adjectives describe positive business attributes, and which do you consider to be negative?

~~intrusive~~	~~dynamic~~	interfering	courteous
energetic	insensitive	perceptive	clumsy
purposeful	discourteous		

Positive attributes

……………… *dynamic* ………………

………………

………………………………………………………

………………………………………………………

………………………………………………………

………………………………………………………

Negative attributes

……………… *intrusive*

………………………………………………………

………………………………………………………

………………………………………………………

………………………………………………………

C

In this next recording, Huilian, from Shanghai in China, describes her experiences of different negotiating styles.

 1 Read through the questions. Then play the recording and note down your answers to check your general understanding of what Huilian says.

1 What is Huilian's job?

2 Who does she negotiate with in her everyday work?

3 In her view, how do negotiations with Japanese companies compare with negotiations with local Chinese companies?

4 What is the key factor which she mentions as being important for Chinese companies?

 2 Now listen again. Stop the recording as necessary, and complete the gaps in these sentences.

1 We have a lot of chances .... with different companies.

2 They will need .... at their headquarter[s].

3 We negotiate with their .... or sales department.

4 In some Chinese companies, we will .... very fast.

5 Maybe some company don't .... on the legal too much.

6 They prefer (to) .... as soon as possible.

 3 Notice the way Huilian speaks and rewrite the following sentences in 'standard' English. Does her accent and pronunciation cause you any difficulties in understanding what she says?

1 They are quite emphasise on the every word.

....

2 They will need to confirm at their headquarter or legal consult.

....

3 So, it's quite be very long.

....

4 Maybe some company don't emphasise on the legal too much.

....

5 They prefer finish this project as soon as possible.

....

FURTHER STUDY

Reflect on any difficulties you have had whilst taking part in negotiations across cultures. Usually, it is not important to catch everything that is said to you in English, but in detailed negotiations, it can be vital that you understand every word, so extensive work on your listening skills is very important.

18 Written and spoken communication

If you wouldn't write it and sign it, don't say it. – Earl Wilson (American journalist, gossip columnist and author)

A

Dylan is a sales manager from Los Angeles. In this recording he is talking to a colleague about the standards of written English which he encounters in his everyday work.

1 Read the questions and then play the recording. Answer the questions to test your general comprehension.

1 In Dylan's view, do his business contacts in Asia consider grammar and spelling to be important?
2 Is he usually sure of the precise meaning of emails which he receives?
3 Would he sign off a business email with emoticons?
4 What is his opinion of ending a business email in this way?

2 Now listen again, pausing when necessary to complete the gaps in the sentences.

1 … where there's lots of consumer electronics industries ………………
2 You become a lot more loose in your … in your ……………… for correct forms.
3 You don't read the …………………………… of it.
4 You just kind of need to interpret it to see what they're ……………… because …
5 And she ……………… with a signature, like an image signature.
6 Not that it's a bad thing. It's ……………… friendly, I guess …

3 In common with most speakers, Dylan uses a lot of 'fillers' when he speaks in order to give himself time to formulate what he wants to say. Listen to the recording again and listen out for the following phrases.

– **Like, I feel like** you kind of …
– You **kind of have to just** accept that …
– **And you know**, you find yourself **not really, you know** …
– **You just kind of** have to interpret it to **kind of** see what …
– She signed it with a signature, **like an** image signature …
– **Like, I just … I just** don't think over on this side of the world …
– It's a cultural thing, **I guess**.

B

Jing is from Wuhan in China. In this recording, she talks about using written and spoken English in her everyday business life.

 1 Read the questions and then play the recording. Answer the questions to test your general understanding.

1 How does she communicate with people in foreign countries?

2 Jing mentions a particular problem she has had with someone from which country?

3 What is her solution to potential misunderstandings?

4 What does she suggest that they can use to find out the exact meaning of one another's emails?

Useful vocabulary and phrases: synchronising time

What's the time where you are?

I'll call you at 5 o'clock CET. (CET = Central European Time)

That's 4 o'clock your time and 7 o'clock in the evening my time.

We're three hours ahead of / behind you.

We need to move our watches forward / back.

Sorry, I got the time for our meeting wrong.

 2 Jing makes a couple of mistakes concerning standard use of articles: 'He's not *a* native English speaker', 'write down the words in *an* email'. Do these cause you any problems in understanding what she says? Now listen again and complete the gaps in the transcript.

So, during the business maybe we have some **1** .... between the foreign countries. For example, sometimes we have to write email(s) or telephone the foreign countries. I remember, once I called a manager in **2** .... Because his English maybe is not very good, because he's not [an] English **3** ...., so his pronunciation maybe is hard for me to **4** .... But then we think, maybe it's better for us to **5** .... the words in [an] email. We can find the words and refer to the dictionary and to **6** .... the exact meaning [of] what he said.

C

Anna works for a global media company based in Glasgow, Scotland. In this recording she describes her day-to-day dealings with her boss in London and with 'external global agencies'.

 1 Read the questions and then play the recording through once and answer the questions to test your general understanding.

1 How often does Anna have a face-to-face meeting with her boss?

2 Does she consider it to be a problem that she is not able to have regular face-to-face meetings?

3   What other methods of communication does she use with her boss?

4   Why does she consider visiting customers and agency staff to be so important?

49

2 **Now listen again. Complete the gaps and note the way that Anna pronounces the following phrases. How does your pronunciation compare with hers?**

1   My direct manager .... in London.

2   There are a few .... in that we don't have face-to-face meetings.

3   Both of us travel .... perhaps ...

4   I think it's important to .... that level of communication.

5   I think as long as people .... to travel, then I see no problem.

6   I think it's important to travel .... to see customers.

7   ... as it .... the partnership and the relationship.

☰ COBUILD CHECK: face-to-face interaction

- *For example, in **face-to-face interaction**, you speak and listen, but you also gesture and receive signals visually.*

- *They tend to place a higher value on **face-to-face conversations** and on phone calls than they do on over-the-Net communication.*

- *I went **in person** to the office and pressed the agent very strongly to accept our offer, which he finally did.*

- *Thanks for your e-mail and I will look forward to meeting you **in the flesh** next Friday morning.*

- *In contrast to **one-to-one** interviews, which are the norm in the private sector, public bodies prefer to put applicants through a series of panel interviews.*

- *The camera lens is on the back of the phone, so it is clearly not intended for **person-to-person** video conferencing.*

Scottish speakers

Scottish people use many words that may be unfamiliar to even their closest neighbours. However, they are unlikely to use most of these in a business environment.

Here are some informal Scottish words and expressions with their 'standard English' equivalents:

I'm running a wee bit late. = I'm running a little late. (*wee* = small/little)

Aye, that's no bother. = Yes, that's no problem.

There are some folk fae New York in the office today. = There are some people from New York in the office today.

I'm awfy busy at the minute. = I'm very busy at the moment.

It's a bonny/bonnie day today. = It's a beautiful day today.

It's a dreich day. = It's a miserable, cold and wet day.

Happy Hogmanay! = Happy New Year! Note: Hogmanay is 31st December, not 1st January.

3 Anna discusses contacts which she has 'on a daily basis' and 'once a month'. Revise expressions of time by completing the phrases with a preposition from the box.

every	since	once	weekly	by	until	in	on

1 We are usually in touch .... a week.

2 We try to arrange a face-to-face meeting .... six weeks.

3 I'll do some checking and I'll email you .... two days' time.

4 I won't be in touch again .... Tuesday week.

5 Please let me have the information .... the end of the week.

6 Let's meet .... Monday morning.

7 I've been based in Hong Kong .... 9th December.

8 We have .... web meetings with each of our external agencies.

Clear usage: talking about time

When was the meeting?

The day before yesterday

Last Friday

The week before last

Three weeks ago

At least six months before that

When is the next meeting?

On Tuesday at 3 o'clock

Next Tuesday

A week on Tuesday / Tuesday week
[these have the same meaning]

In three weeks' time

At the end of the month

FURTHER STUDY

Do you prefer to make phone calls, to use email or instant messaging or do you make time for face-to-face meetings? Think about when communication has gone wrong. Look through trails of emails. Have you had similar experiences to Dylan when receiving emails from around the world? Would you use emoticons when writing a business email? What are the key issues for you when speaking or writing in English?

For further recordings, including more from Dylan, go to the website **www.collinselt.com/businesslistening.**

19 Meeting and greeting

You never get a second chance to make a good first impression.
– Hannah Tatum Whitall Smith (American author)

A   Cristobalina is Spanish but has lived in the UK for two years so her Spanish accent has some London influences. In this recording, she compares the way people meet and greet each other in Spain and in London.

1   Read the questions and then play the recording through once. Answer the questions to check your general comprehension.

1   In Spain, who might you kiss on the cheek the first time you meet?
2   Would you normally kiss a new business acquaintance on the first meeting?
3   What reason does she give for people in London kissing each other on the cheek when meeting?
4   In her view, under what circumstances would people hug each other?

2   Now listen again, stop the recording as necessary, and complete the gaps in the sentences.

1   If it's like [a] friend of [a] friend ……………….……… them on the cheek.
2   In a business environment you're ……………… kiss them on the cheek.
3   At the beginning they … some of them …………..…………… a little bit.
4   We are open and for us feeling, ………….…………..……… is very important.
5   People kiss on (in) ………………, you know, more and more in London.
6   Maybe (the) ………………....………….… is more when you know someone.

⬚ COBUILD CHECK: describing behaviour

- They have a basically positive attitude and are **warm**, friendly, kind and **supportive** towards others.

- The managers are media-trained to be bland and **inoffensive** in interviews.

- Service is impeccable and the staff are extremely **polite**.

- His friendly persona is a useful negotiating tool – it wouldn't do to appear too **threatening**.

- In decades of multilateral negotiations, we've never experienced this kind of **insulting** behaviour.

- Managers used to free-flowing kinds of interviews are likely to view structured interviews as **cold** and **impersonal**.

- At times you are **extroverted**, **easy-going**, and **sociable**, while at other times you are **introverted**, **wary**, and **reserved**.

3 Cristobalina and the other speakers in this unit discuss greetings behaviour which, in some cultures, may be seen as appropriate but in others would be inappropriate or even shocking. Select adjectives from the box which suggest appropriate and inappropriate behaviour and write them into the correct list.

threatening	respectful	insulting	reassuring
overbearing	warm	welcoming	easy-going
rude	impolite	cold	polite
hostile	supportive	offensive	professional

'Appropriate' behaviour

....

....

....

....

....

....

....

....

'Inappropriate' behaviour

....

....

....

....

....

....

....

....

B

Andrea is from Italy and works in a company in London which has employees from many countries. In this recording, he talks about how Italian people like to meet, greet, and have fun.

1 Read the general comprehension questions below. Then, play the recording through once and answer the questions.

1 According to Andrea, are Italian people generally sociable?

2 Which part of Italy is he from?

3 How does he usually greet his friends?

4 Does he greet male and female friends in the same way?

5 Why does he believe that he cannot always 'be himself' when he is in London?

2 Notice the way Andrea says the following. Underline any words and phrases which you find difficult to understand.

– I think Italian people is really people with a good fantasy [= imagination].

– We enjoy to be together, to organise also dinner— restaurants together.

– Sometimes, for people from other countries, those things could be too much.

- But in this country, if I kiss one guy, for example – just a friend – people can think something about my sexual orientation.
- I cannot express myself in one hundred per cents – totally.

> Note that Andrea says: 'Italian people is really people …' 'Standard' English would be: *Italian people* **are** …
> He says: 'We enjoy to be together'. 'Standard' English would be: *We enjoy* **being** *together.*
> He says: 'When I meet a friends …' 'Standard' English would be: *When I meet* **a friend** …
> He says: 'If I kiss one guy …' 'Standard' English would be: *If I kiss* **a guy** …
> He says: 'I cannot express myself one hundred per cents.' 'Standard' English would be: *one hundred per cent.*

3 **Play the recording again. Pause it as necessary to complete the gaps in the phrases and sentences.**

1 We are really .... people.

2 Those things could be too much because they are not .... us.

3 It's common when I meet a friends (a friend) just to .... him or her.

4 For me, it's really strange. I need to .... myself.

5 I cannot .... (in) one hundred per cents (one hundred per cent).

4 **Which of these forms of greeting are familiar to you when meeting business acquaintances, close friends, family? Which of them would make you feel uncomfortable from a point of view of them being too cold or too intimate?**

- A kiss on one cheek
- A kiss on both cheeks
- A kiss on the lips
- Holding someone's shoulders
- Hugging
- Bowing
- Shaking hands
- Just smiling
- Simply making eye-contact

Useful vocabulary and phrases: informal greetings

Have you met our new sales coordinator, Carlos Saares?

It's great to meet you at last.

And you.

And this is Fernando Benitez.

Hello / Hi, Fernando. I've heard a lot about you.

Let me give you my card?

Thanks. Here's mine.

C

Catrina, who is from Canada, makes some comments on meeting and greeting habits in the Middle East and Asia.

1 Read the questions and then play the recording. Are these statements true or false?

	True	False
1 The majority of people working in Catrina's office are men.		
2 Most of their clients in the Middle East are men.		
3 Catrina says it is not considered appropriate for women to shake hands with men when they are in the Middle East.		
4 It is considered rude to hand over a business card with two hands in Asia.		

2 Listen again. Pause the recording as necessary and complete the gaps in the phrases and sentences.

1 When my .... have to go to the Middle East …

2 When they go to the Middle East, for example, they're .... shake hands with the men.

3 All of their clients .... (typically) male.

4 There are little, just the little .... of business culture in Asia …

5 It's quite rude to .... a business card with one hand.

⬚ COBUILD CHECK: greetings and gestures

- Subtle **nuances** from specific traditions can, unfortunately, be lost in translation.

- Be very alert to posture, **gestures**, facial expressions, and the tone and inflection in the speaker's voice.

- For most conversations people tend to feel comfortable with **eye contact** for about fifty per cent of the time.

- She **kissed** them lightly on both cheeks, a traditional Brazilian greeting.

- We **shook hands** civilly, even though this was an awkward situation for both of us.

- As the bus pulled away from the bus stop at Kansai, the baggage handlers lined up and **bowed** politely.

- Friends and strangers **hugged** and toasted, wishing each other Happy New Year.

- If you should catch his eye as you pass, he will **acknowledge** you with a courteous nod.

FURTHER STUDY

For further recordings, go to **www.collinselt.com/businesslistening.**

20 Working hours and the office environment

I've created an atmosphere where I'm a friend first, boss second, probably entertainer third. – David Brent (character in comedy series, The Office)

A

In this recording, Cristobalina, who is from Jerez de la Frontera, a city in Andalusia in the south of Spain, talks about typical Spanish working hours.

53

1 Read the questions and then play the recording. Are these statements true or false?

	True	False
1 Working hours are fairly standard across a range of businesses and industries in Spain.		
2 She enjoys taking a siesta.		
3 She prefers to work eight hours in a row with only a short break for lunch.		
4 She likes to finish early in the day so that she has time for herself and her family.		

53

2 Now listen again. Notice the way that Cristobalina pronounces the following words and phrases. Underline any particular phrases which you had difficulty in understanding when you first listened to the recording.

- Certain kind of businesses in Spain, like travel agencies … Then you have one or two hours for lunch …
- You finish early and you have the rest of the day.
- It depends on the business that you're in.
- If you work in a hotel, that's fine.
- You do a late shift, which leaves you the morning free.

> Cristobalina says: 'They normally used to work maybe eight to one.'
> Standard English would be: *They are normally used to working (from) maybe eight to one.*

Clear usage: describing everyday work patterns

Cristobalina describes everyday work patterns very clearly using the simple present tense:

'Then you have to go back to the office.'

'If you work in a hotel, that's fine.'

'You do a shift and work quite early in the morning.'

'You finish at three.'

'You do a late shift which leaves you the morning free.'

☰ COBUILD CHECK: working hours

- *There have been various attempts to **stagger** working hours.*

- *When we started in the factory we used to have some weekend **overtime** but then it was cancelled.*

- *The nurses are working 12-hour **shifts** without a proper break.*

- *Most 'sleep experts' say that the **siesta** is good for the heart.*

- *The strikers are demanding higher pay and better **working conditions**.*

- *He started his **working life** as a truck driver.*

- *Short-term contracts and **flexible** working are becoming easier to arrange.*

---

3 Match the words on the left with words on the right to complete the phrase. Check the definitions of any unfamiliar terms in the Mini-dictionary towards the back of this book.

1	weekly	a	ban
2	overtime	b	break
3	coffee	c	shift patterns
4	staggered	d	conditions
5	poor working	e	period
6	rest	f	lunch breaks

'Spanglish'

Siesta is one of many words which have come into the English language from Spanish. Here are some others:

cafeteria (from *cafeteria*)

cargo (from *cargar,* 'to load')

macho (*macho* usually means simply 'male' in Spanish)

potato (from *patata* and *batata*)

pronto (from an adjective or adverb meaning 'soon', 'quick' or 'quickly')

salsa (a general word for 'sauce' in Spanish)

tomato (from *tomate*)

tornado (from *tronada,* thunderstorm)

tuna (from *atún*)

B

Andrea is from southern Italy. In this recording he gives his impressions of working in a multicultural office environment.

1 Read the questions and then play the recording once. Answer the questions to test your general understanding.

1 Which other nationalities work on the 'Italian island'?

2 What kind of world do you see when you walk into the office and look left?

3 What kind of world do you see when you walk into the office and look right?

4 What nationality is his boss?

5 Why does Andrea believe that the Japanese side of the office is so quiet? (Do you agree with him?)

6 What emotion does he believe that his Japanese friends and colleagues 'have inside'?

2 **Now listen again, stop the recording as necessary, and complete the gaps in the sentences.**

1 My office .... in two parts.

2 Just imagine (the) ...., open the door ...

3 At the end of the month we are really ....

4 Everyone is happy, everyone is .... in the office.

5 The other half of the office is quite ....

6 In our half you cannot hear the .... of a storm outside because we are the storm inside.

7 During also the private life [In their private life], they .... the same way.

Note what Andrea says and the equivalent in 'standard' English

'hells' = hell

'It's really professional office.' = It's a really professional office.

'The Japanese guy I used to live in Italy ...' = The Japanese guy I used to live with in Italy ...

'He replied me' = He replied to me/He replied/He told me

'Are you feel well?' = Do you feel okay? or Are you feeling okay?

'Italian people is totally opposite.' = Italian people are totally the opposite. / Italian people are the complete opposite.

---

3 **Put the words in the box into the left hand list if you believe they relate to an 'organised' office and into the right hand list if they relate to a 'disorganised' office.**

cluttered	uncluttered	~~organised~~	chaotic	muddled
messy	neat	ordered	calm	~~disorganised~~

.... *organised* .... *disorganised* ....

....

....

....

....

☰ COBUILD CHECK: the office environment

- His office was so **cluttered** that he often preferred to conduct media interviews elsewhere.

- Reserved by nature, they frown on loud or **boisterous** public behaviour.

- Workers in jobs that are **stressful** and **hectic** with heavy workloads and conflicting demands don't consider their work environments to be healthy.

- I wanted to stay with the company because it had a very **lively** atmosphere, but not doing the same thing for ever.

- Ice-breakers are useful if you want to create a warm and **relaxed** atmosphere which will help foster discussion groups.

- She first asks bosses to visualise what a **stress-free** working environment would be like.

- The report showed that despite working longer hours, Britain's workers are still less **productive** than those in the US and Europe.

- He seemed impressed by my devotion to keeping the place **spick and span**.

C

Marcello is a catering manager from Port Elizabeth in South Africa. In this short recording he talks about his staff's working hours.

1 Read the questions. Then play the recording and answer these questions to check your general comprehension.

   1 How many hours does the first part-time girl work?

   2 What time does the second part-timer leave work?

   3 What are Marcello's working hours?

   4 What time do the chefs come to work?

   5 What do the chefs have to do before they leave work?

2 Listen again. Pause the recording as necessary and complete the gaps in the sentences:

   1 At the moment we have two girls that work ....

   2 So one comes in at .... in the morning.

   3 The other one .... where she leaves off.

   4 I work from eight until ...., same as Carl.

   5 The chefs ... they come in at seven .... three-thirty.

   6 ... they've cleaned up and everything's .... and then ...

FURTHER STUDY

Now listen to the recordings in this unit again and study the transcripts. If you work with Spanish, Italian or South African speakers of English, ask them if you can record your conversations and analyse them to improve your comprehension.

For further recordings, including more from Marcello as he talks about his South African biltong business, go to the website **www.collinselt.com/businesslistening.**

MINI-DICTIONARY

 Some of the most difficult words from each unit are defined here in this Mini-dictionary. The definitions are extracts from the *Collins COBUILD Advanced Dictionary* and focus on the meanings of the words in the contexts in which they appear in the book.

Unit 1

ac|ro|nym N-COUNT An **acronym** is a word composed of the first letters of the words in a phrase, especially when this is used as a name. An example of an acronym is NATO which is made up of the first letters of the 'North Atlantic Treaty Organization'.

clause N-COUNT In grammar, a **clause** is a group of words containing a verb. Sentences contain one or more clauses. There are finite clauses and non-finite clauses.

col|lo|quial ADJ **Colloquial** words and phrases are informal and are used mainly in conversation. • *...a colloquial expression.*

dia|lect N-VAR A **dialect** is a form of a language that is spoken in a particular area. • *In the fifties, many Italians spoke only local dialect.*

in|to|na|tion N-VAR Your **intonation** is the way that your voice rises and falls as you speak.

mel|low VERB If someone **mellows** or if something **mellows** them, they become kinder or less extreme in their behaviour.

ob|sta|cle N-COUNT You can refer to anything that makes it difficult for you to do something as an **obstacle**. • *Overcrowding remains a large obstacle to improving conditions.*

posh ADJ If you describe a person as **posh**, you mean that they belong to or behave as if they belong to the upper classes. *(informal)* • *He sounded so posh on the phone.*

Unit 2

ap|plaud VERB When an attitude or action **is applauded**, people praise it. • *She applauds the fact that they are promoting new ideas.*

blur|ry ADJ A **blurry** shape is one that has an unclear outline.

break into If someone **breaks into** something they suddenly start doing it. For example, if someone **breaks into** a run they suddenly start running.

in|roads PHRASE If one thing **makes inroads into** another, the first thing starts affecting or destroying the second.

make out If you **make** something **out**, you manage with difficulty to see or hear it. • *I heard the voices, but couldn't make out what they were saying.*

Unit 3

in|va|lid ADJ If an action, procedure, or document is **invalid**, it cannot be accepted, because it breaks the law or some official rule. • *We cannot accept liability if you are refused entry because of invalid documents.*

make up for To **make up for** a bad experience or the loss of something means to make the situation better or make the person involved happier. • *Ask for an extra compensation payment to make up for the stress you have been caused.*

out|stand|ing ADJ Money that is **outstanding** has not yet been paid and is still owed to someone. • *You have to pay your outstanding bill before joining the scheme.*

que|ry VERB If you **query** something, you check it by asking about it because you are not sure if it is correct. • *It's got a number you can ring to query your bill.*

Unit 5

stretch PHRASE If you say that something is not true or possible **by any stretch of the imagination**, you are emphasizing that it is completely untrue or absolutely impossible.

dis|arm|ing ADJ If someone or something is **disarming**, they make you feel less angry or hostile.

em|broiled ADJ If you become **embroiled in** a fight or argument, you become deeply involved in it.

fran|tic ADJ If an activity is **frantic**, things are done quickly and in an energetic but disorganized way, because there is very little time. • *A busy night in the restaurant can be frantic in the kitchen.*

off|set VERB If one thing **is offset** by another, the effect of the first thing is reduced by the second, so that any advantage or disadvantage is cancelled out. • *The increase in pay costs was offset by higher productivity.*

sanc|tu|ary N-COUNT A **sanctuary** is a place where people who are in danger from other people can go to be safe.

scrub N-UNCOUNT **Scrub** consists of low trees and bushes, especially in an area that has very little rain. • *...an area of scrub and woodland.*

stance N-COUNT Your **stance** on a particular matter is your attitude to it. • *They have maintained a consistently neutral stance.*

weight N-VAR If something is given a particular **weight**, it is given a particular value according to how important or significant it is. • *The scientists involved put different weight on the conclusions of different models.*

Unit 6

al|ien ADJ If something is **alien to** you or **to** your normal feelings or behaviour, it is not the way you would normally feel or behave. *(formal)* • *Such an attitude is alien to most businessmen.*

hail VERB Someone who **hails from** a particular place was born there or lives there. *(formal)* • *I hail from Brighton.*

in|hib|it VERB If something **inhibits** an event or process, it prevents it or slows it down. • *The high cost of borrowing is inhibiting investment by industry in new equipment.*

ini|ti|ate VERB If you **initiate** something, you start it or cause it to happen. • *They wanted to initiate a discussion on economics.*

liq|ui|date VERB To **liquidate** a company is to close it down and sell all its assets, usually because it is in debt. • **liq|ui|da|tion** N-VAR • *The company went into liquidation.*

con|tr|ary PHRASE You use **on the contrary** when you have just said or implied that something is not true and are going to say that the opposite is true. • *It is not an idea around which we can unite. On the contrary, I see it as one that will divide us.*

Do not confuse **on the contrary** with **on the other hand**. **On the contrary** is used to contradict someone, to say that they are wrong. **On the other hand** is used to state a different, often contrasting aspect of the situation you are considering. *Prices of consumer goods fell. Wages on the other hand increased.*

dole PHRASE Someone who is **on the dole** is registered as unemployed and receives money from the government. *(mainly Brit)* • *It's not easy living on the dole.*

in AM, usually use **on welfare**

over|ly ADV **Overly** means more than is normal, necessary, or reasonable. • *Employers may become overly cautious about taking on new staff.*

pre|requi|site N-COUNT If one thing is a **prerequisite for** another, it must happen or exist before the other thing is possible. • *Good self-esteem is a prerequisite for a happy life.*

re|luc|tant ADJ If you are **reluctant to** do something, you are unwilling to do it and hesitate before doing it, or do it slowly and without enthusiasm. • *Mr Spero was reluctant to ask for help.*

aback PHRASE If you are **taken aback by** something, you are surprised or shocked by it and you cannot respond at once. • *Roland was taken aback by our strength of feeling.*

Unit 7

bar|ren ADJ A **barren** landscape is dry and bare, and has very few plants and no trees.

di|verse ADJ **Diverse** people or things are very different from each other. • *Jones has a much more diverse and perhaps younger audience.*

giv|en PHRASE If you say **given that** something is the case, you mean taking that fact into account.

• *Usually, I am sensible with money, as I have to be, given that I don't earn that much.*

launch VERB To **launch** a large and important activity, for example a military attack, means to start it. • *The police have launched an investigation into the incident.*

lush ADJ **Lush** fields or gardens have a lot of very healthy grass or plants. • *... the lush green meadows bordering the river.*

per|cep|tion N-COUNT Your **perception of** something is the way that you think about it or the impression you have of it.

pro|fes|sion|al|ism N-UNCOUNT **Professionalism** in a job is a combination of skill and high standards. • *There was a lack of professionalism in their dealings.*

ter|rain N-VAR **Terrain** is used to refer to an area of land or a type of land when you are considering its physical features. • *The terrain changed quickly from arable land to desert.*

Unit 8

cred|ibil|ity N-UNCOUNT If someone or something has **credibility**, people believe in them and trust them. • *The president will have to work hard to restore his credibility.*

dif|fer|en|ti|ate VERB If you **differentiate between** things or if you **differentiate** one thing **from** another, you recognize or show the difference between them. • *A child may not differentiate between his imagination and the real world.*

di|verse ADJ If a group or range of things is diverse, it is made up of a wide variety of things. • *Society is now much more diverse than ever before.*

guts N-UNCOUNT **Guts** is the will and courage to do something which is difficult or unpleasant, or which might have unpleasant results. *(informal)* • *The new Chancellor has the guts to push through unpopular tax increases.*

im|mi|nent ADJ If you say that something is **imminent**, especially something unpleasant, you mean it is almost certain to happen very soon. • *They warned that an attack is imminent.*

ploy N-COUNT A **ploy** is a way of behaving that someone plans carefully and secretly in order to gain an advantage for themselves.

scat|ter VERB If a group of people **scatter** or if you **scatter** them, they suddenly separate and move in different directions. • *After dinner, everyone scattered.*

trust|worthy ADJ A **trustworthy** person is reliable, responsible, and can be trusted completely. • *He is a trustworthy and level-headed leader.*

Unit 9

bar|ri|er N-COUNT A **barrier** is something such as a fence or wall that is put in place to prevent people from moving easily from one area to another.

com|mute VERB If you **commute**, you travel a long distance every day between your home and your place of work. • *Mike commutes to London every day.* • **com|mut|er** N-COUNT • *The number of commuters to London has dropped by 100,000.* • *...a commuter train.*

pro|cure|ment N-UNCOUNT **Procurement** is the act of obtaining something such as supplies for an army or other organization. *(formal)*

shut|tle N-COUNT A **shuttle** is a plane, bus, or train which makes frequent journeys between two places. • *...the BA shuttle to Glasgow.*

sup|posed PHRASE If something **was supposed to** happen, it was planned or intended to happen, but did not in fact happen. • *The first debate was supposed to have been held on Tuesday.*

Unit 10

cole|slaw N-UNCOUNT **Coleslaw** is a salad of chopped raw cabbage, carrots, onions, and sometimes other vegetables, usually with mayonnaise.

cool|er N-COUNT A **cooler** is a container for keeping things cool, especially drinks.

cul|ti|vate VERB If you **cultivate** someone or **cultivate** a friendship with them, you try hard to develop a friendship with them.

high-profile ADJ A **high-profile** person or a **high-profile** event attracts a lot of attention or publicity.

hos|pi|tal|ity N-UNCOUNT **Hospitality** is the food, drink, and other privileges which some companies provide for their visitors or clients at major sporting or other public events.

pro|spec|tive ADJ You use **prospective** to describe someone who wants to be the thing mentioned or who is likely to be the thing mentioned. • *The story should act as a warning to other prospective buyers.*

sip N-COUNT A **sip** is a small amount of drink that you take into your mouth. • *Katherine took another sip from her glass to calm herself.*

woo VERB If you **woo** people, you try to encourage them to help you, support you, or vote for you, for example by promising them things which they would like. • *They wooed customers by offering low interest rates.*

Unit 11

bland ADJ Food that is **bland** has very little flavour. • *It tasted bland and insipid, like warmed cardboard.*

broil VERB When you **broil** food, you cook it using very strong heat directly above or below it. *(Am)* • *I'll broil the lobster.*

in BRIT, use **grill**

chewy ADJ If food is **chewy**, it needs to be chewed a lot before it becomes soft enough to swallow. • *The meat was too chewy.*

crunchy ADJ Food that is **crunchy** is pleasantly hard or crisp so that it makes a noise when you eat it. • *... fresh, crunchy vegetables.*

gris|tle N-UNCOUNT **Gristle** is a tough, rubbery substance found in meat, especially in meat of poor quality, which is unpleasant to eat.

lean ADJ If meat is **lean**, it does not have very much fat. • *It is a beautiful meat, very lean and tender.*

mari|nade N-COUNT A **marinade** is a sauce of oil, vinegar, spices, and herbs, which you pour over meat or fish before you cook it, in order to add flavour, or to make the meat or fish softer.

poach VERB When you **poach** an egg, you cook it gently in boiling water without its shell. • *He had a light breakfast of poached eggs and tea.*

sea|son|ing N-VAR **Seasoning** is salt, pepper, or other spices that are added to food to improve its flavour. • *Mix the meat with the onion, carrot, and some seasoning.*

spit N-UNCOUNT A **spit** is a long rod which is pushed through a piece of meat and hung over an open fire to cook the meat. • *She roasted the meat on a spit.*

Unit 12

ap|pre|ci|ate VERB If you **appreciate** a situation or problem, you understand it and know what it involves. • *He appreciates that co-operation with the media is part of his professional duties.*

cri|teri|on (criteria) N-COUNT A **criterion** is a factor on which you judge or decide something. • *The most important criterion for entry is that applicants must design and make their own work.*

dreary ADJ If you describe something as **dreary**, you mean that it is dull and depressing. • *They live such dreary lives.*

has|sle N-VAR A **hassle** is a situation that is difficult and involves problems, effort, or arguments with people. (informal) • *...a day spent travelling, with all the usual hassles at airport check-in.*

le|thar|gic ADJ If you are **lethargic**, you do not have much energy or enthusiasm. • *He felt too miserable and lethargic to get dressed.*

per|sis|tent ADJ Someone who is **persistent** continues trying to do something, even though it is difficult or other people are against it. • *He phoned again this morning. He's very persistent.*

put up with If you **put up with** something, you tolerate or accept it, even though you find it unpleasant or unsatisfactory. • *They had put up with behaviour from their son which they would not have tolerated from anyone else.*

re|luc|tant ADJ If you are **reluctant to** do something, you are unwilling to do it and hesitate before doing it, or do it slowly and without enthusiasm. • *Mr Spero was reluctant to ask for help.*

slug|gish ADJ You can describe something as **sluggish** if it moves, works, or reacts much slower than you would like or is normal. • *The economy remains sluggish.*

stipu|late VERB If you **stipulate** a condition or **stipulate that** something must be done, you say clearly that it must be done. • *She could have stipulated that she would pay when she collected the computer.*

te|na|cious ADJ If you are **tenacious**, you are very determined and do not give up easily. • *She is very tenacious and will work hard and long to achieve objectives.*

tube N-SING **The tube** is the underground railway system in London. (Brit) • *I took the tube then the train and came straight here.*

tricky ADJ If you describe a task or problem as **tricky**, you mean that it is difficult to do or deal with. • *Parking can be tricky in the town centre.*

wreck VERB To **wreck** something means to completely destroy or ruin it.

Unit 13

af|fair N-COUNT If two people who are not married to each other have an **affair**, they have a sexual relationship. • *She was having an affair with someone at work.*

back-stab|bing N-UNCOUNT **Back-stabbing** consists of unkind and disloyal actions or remarks that are likely to harm someone such as a friend or colleague. • *She accused her colleagues of bullying and back-stabbing.*

groom VERB If you **are groomed for** a special job, someone prepares you for it by teaching you the skills you will need. • *George was already being groomed for the top job.*

in|duc|tion N-VAR **Induction** is a procedure or ceremony for introducing someone to a new job, organization, or way of life. • *...an induction course for new members.*

land VERB If you **land** something that is difficult to get and that many people want, you are successful in getting it. (informal) • *He landed a place on the graduate training scheme.*

lob|by N-COUNT In a hotel or other large building, the **lobby** is the area near the entrance that usually has corridors and staircases leading off it. • *I met her in the lobby of the museum.*

pre|cede VERB If one event or period of time **precedes** another, it happens before it. (formal) • *Industrial orders had already fallen in the preceding months.*

sub|si|dize

in BRIT, also use **subsidise**

VERB If a government or other authority **subsidizes** something, they pay part of the cost of it. • *At the moment they are existing on pensions that are subsidised by the government.*

up|keep N-UNCOUNT The **upkeep** of a building or place is the work of keeping it in good condition. • *The maintenance department is responsible for the general upkeep of the park.*

Unit 14

ac|cru|al (accruals) N-COUNT In finance, the **accrual** of something such as interest or investments is the adding together of interest or different investments over a period of time. • *...the accrual of funds used during construction.* • *...an accrual method of accounting.*

ac|crue VERB If money or interest **accrues** or if you **accrue** it, it gradually increases in amount over a period of time. • *If you do not pay within 28 days, interest will accrue.*

audi|tor N-COUNT An **auditor** is an accountant who officially examines the accounts of organizations.

bal|ance sheet N-COUNT A **balance sheet** is a written statement of the amount of money and property that a company or person has, including amounts of money that are owed or are owing. **Balance sheet** is also used to refer to the general financial state of a company. • *Rolls-Royce needed a strong balance sheet.*

de|rive VERB If you say that something such as a word or feeling **derives** or **is derived from** something else, you mean that it comes from that thing.

en|sure VERB To **ensure** something, or to **ensure that** something happens, means to make certain that it happens. (formal) • *Ensure that it is written into your contract.*

ex|ecute VERB If you **execute** a plan, you carry it out. (formal) • *We are going to execute our campaign plan to the letter.*

fraud N-VAR **Fraud** is the crime of gaining money or financial benefits by a trick or by lying. • *He was jailed for two years for fraud and deception.*

nitty-gritty also **nitty gritty** N-SING If people get down to **the nitty-gritty** of a matter, situation, or activity, they discuss the most important, basic parts of it or facts about it. (informal) • *The city's newspapers still attempt to get down to the nitty gritty of investigative journalism.*

over|heads N-PLURAL The **overheads** of a business are its regular and essential expenses, such as salaries, rent, electricity, and telephone bills. • *We are having to cut our costs to reduce overheads and remain competitive.*

sev|er|ance ADJ **Severance** pay is a sum of money that a company gives to its employees when it has to stop employing them. • *We were offered 13 weeks' severance pay.*

stake|hold|er N-COUNT **Stakeholders** are people who have an interest in a company's or organization's affairs.

stock|hold|er N-COUNT A **stockholder** is a person who owns shares in a company. (Am)

in BRIT, use **shareholder**

trans|ac|tion N-COUNT A **transaction** is a piece of business, for example an act of buying or selling something. (formal)

Unit 15

ad|equate ADJ If something is **adequate**, there is enough of it or it is good enough to be used or accepted. • *The old methods weren't adequate to meet current needs.* • **ad|equate|ly** ADV • *Many students are not adequately prepared for higher education.* • *I speak the language adequately.*

buoy|ant ADJ A **buoyant** economy is a successful one in which there is a lot of trade and economic activity. • *High interest rates do not point to a buoyant market this year.* • *Analysts expect the share price to remain buoyant.*

cush|ion VERB To **cushion** the effect of something unpleasant means to reduce it. • *The subsidies are designed to cushion farmers against unpredictable weather.*

en|ti|tle VERB If you **are entitled to** something, you have the right to have it or do it. • *If the warranty is limited, the terms may entitle you to a replacement or refund.*

head|hunt VERB If someone who works for a particular company **is headhunted**, they leave that company because another company has approached them and offered them another job with better pay and higher status. • *He was headhunted by Barkers last October to build an advertising team.*

in|evi|table ADJ If something is **inevitable**, it is certain to happen and cannot be prevented or avoided. • *If the case succeeds, it is inevitable that other trials will follow.*

lay|off N-COUNT When there are **layoffs** in a company, workers are told by their employers to leave their job, usually because there is no more work for them in the company. • *It will close more than 200 stores nationwide resulting in the layoffs of an estimated 2,000 employees.*

line up If you **line up** an event or activity, you arrange for it to happen. If you **line** someone **up** for an event or activity, you arrange for them to be available for that event or activity. • *She lined up executives, politicians and educators to serve on the board of directors.*

no|tice N-UNCOUNT If you give **notice** about something that is going to happen, you give a warning in advance that it is going to happen. • *Unions are required to give seven days' notice of industrial action.* • *She was transferred without notice.*

re|ces|sion N-VAR A **recession** is a period when the economy of a country is doing badly, for example because industry is producing less and more people are becoming unemployed. • *The recession caused sales to drop off.*

sack VERB If your employers **sack** you, they tell you that you can no longer work for them because you have done something that they did not like or because your work was not good enough. (Brit) • *Earlier today the Prime Minister sacked 18 government officials for corruption.* • N-SING **Sack** is also a noun. • *People who make mistakes can be given the sack the same day.*

sac|ri|fice VERB If you **sacrifice** something that is valuable or important, you give it up, usually to obtain something else for yourself or for other people. • *She sacrificed family life to her career.* N-VAR • **Sacrifice** is also a noun. • *He was willing to make any sacrifice for peace.*

statu|tory ADJ **Statutory** means relating to rules or laws which have been formally written down. (formal)

• We had a statutory duty to report to Parliament.

Unit 16

blow-by-blow ADJ A **blow-by-blow** account of an event describes every stage of it in great detail. *(informal)* • *She wanted a blow-by-blow account of what happened.*

idio|syn|cra|sy N-VAR If you talk about the **idiosyncrasies** of someone or something, you are referring to their rather unusual habits or characteristics. • *Everyone has a few little idiosyncrasies.*

ir|rel|evant ADJ If you describe something such as a fact or remark as **irrelevant**, you mean that it is not connected with what you are discussing or dealing with. • *The court decided that their testimony would be irrelevant to the case.*

PA N-COUNT A **PA** is the same as a **personal assistant**.

prem|ise N-PLURAL The **premises** of a business or an institution are all the buildings and land that it occupies in one place. • *The business moved to premises in Brompton Road.*

turn out If something **turns out** a particular way, it happens in that way or has the result or degree of success indicated. • *Sometimes things don't turn out the way we think they're going to.*

Unit 17

abide by If you **abide by** a law, agreement, or decision, you do what it says you should do. • *They have got to abide by the rules.*

clum|sy ADJ A **clumsy** person moves or handles things in a careless, awkward way, often so that things

are knocked over or broken. • *Unfortunately, I was still very clumsy behind the wheel of the jeep.*

contra|vene VERB To **contravene** a law or rule means to do something that is forbidden by the law or rule. *(formal)* • *He said the article did not contravene the industry's code of conduct.*

cour|teous ADJ Someone who is **courteous** is polite and respectful to other people. • *He was a kind and courteous man.*

dis|miss VERB When an employer **dismisses** an employee, the employer tells the employee that they are no longer needed to do the job that they have been doing.

flout VERB If you **flout** something such as a law, an order, or an accepted way of behaving, you deliberately do not obey it or follow it. • *Building regulations have been habitually flouted.*

in|cen|tive N-VAR If something is an **incentive to** do something, it encourages you to do it. • *There is little or no incentive to adopt such measures.*

in|dis|creet ADJ If you describe someone as **indiscreet**, you mean that they do or say things in public which they should only do or say secretly or in private.

in|sen|si|tive ADJ If you describe someone as **insensitive**, you are criticizing them for being unaware of or unsympathetic to other people's feelings..

in|tru|sive ADJ Something that is **intrusive** disturbs your mood or your life in a way you do not like. • *Staff are courteous but never intrusive.*

per|cep|tion N-COUNT Your **perception of** something is the way that you think about it or the impression you have of it. • *He is interested in how our perceptions of death affect the way we live.*

per|cep|tive ADJ If you describe a person or their remarks or thoughts as **perceptive**, you think that they are

good at noticing or realizing things, especially things that are not obvious. • *He was one of the most perceptive U.S. political commentators.*

tact|less ADJ If you describe someone as **tactless**, you think what they say or do is likely to offend other people. • *He had alienated many people with his tactless remarks.*

vola|tile ADJ If someone is **volatile**, their mood often changes quickly. • *He has a volatile temper.*

Unit 18

con|straint N-COUNT A **constraint** is something that limits or controls what you can do. • *Their decision to abandon the trip was made because of financial constraints.*

emo|ti|con N-COUNT An **emoticon** is a symbol used in e-mail to show how someone is feeling. :-) is an emoticon showing happiness.

flesh PHRASE If you meet or see someone **in the flesh**, you actually meet or see them, rather than, for example, seeing them in a film or on television. • *You're smaller in the flesh than you look on TV.*

so|lidi|fy VERB If something such as a position or opinion **solidifies**, or if something **solidifies** it, it becomes firmer and more definite and unlikely to change. • *Her behaviour this week has solidified her support within the Department of Justice.*

Unit 19

ac|knowl|edge VERB If you **acknowledge** someone, for example by moving your head or smiling, you show that you have seen and recognized them. • *He saw her but refused to even acknowledge her.*

ap|pro|pri|ate ADJ Something that is **appropriate** is suitable or acceptable for a particular situation. • *Dress neatly and attractively in an outfit appropriate to the job.*

awk|ward ADJ An **awkward** situation is embarrassing and difficult to deal with. • *I was the first to ask him awkward questions but there'll be harder ones to come.*

bland ADJ If you describe someone or something as **bland**, you mean that they are rather dull and unexciting. • *It sounds like an advert: easy on the ear but bland and forgettable.*

bow VERB When you **bow to** someone, you briefly bend your body towards them as a formal way of greeting them or showing respect.

civ|il ADJ Someone who is **civil** is polite in a formal way, but not particularly friendly. *(formal)* • *As visitors, the least we can do is be civil to the people in their own land.*

extro|vert|ed ADJ Someone who is **extroverted** is very active, lively, and friendly. *(mainly Am)* • *Some young people who were easy-going and extroverted as children become self-conscious in early adolescence.*

in BRIT, usually use **extrovert**

ges|ture N-COUNT A **gesture** is a movement that you make with a part of your body, especially your hands, to express emotion or information. • *He throws his hands open in a gesture which clearly indicates his relief.*

im|pec|cable ADJ If you describe something such as someone's behaviour or appearance as **impeccable**, you are emphasizing that it is perfect and has no faults. • *Her academic credentials are impeccable.*

in|ap|pro|pri|ate ADJ If you say that someone's speech or behaviour in a

particular situation is **inappropriate**, you are criticizing it because you think it is not suitable for that situation. • *I feel the remark was inappropriate for such a serious issue.*

in|of|fen|sive ADJ If you describe someone or something as **inoffensive**, you mean that they are not unpleasant or unacceptable in any way, but are perhaps rather dull. • *It's a very nice song. Catchy, and inoffensive.*

in|sult|ing ADJ Something that is **insulting** is rude or offensive. • *One of the apprentices made an insulting remark to a passing officer.*

intro|vert|ed ADJ **Introverted** people are quiet and shy and find it difficult to talk to other people. • *Machen was a lonely, introverted child.*

multi|lat|er|al ADJ **Multilateral** means involving at least three different groups of people or nations.

nod VERB If you **nod**, you bend your head once, as a way of saying hello or goodbye. • *They nodded goodnight to the security man.*

nu|ance N-VAR A **nuance** is a small difference in sound, feeling, appearance, or meaning. • *We can use our eyes and facial expressions to communicate virtually every subtle nuance of emotion there is.*

over|bear|ing ADJ An **overbearing** person tries to make other people do what he or she wants in an unpleasant and forceful way. • *My husband can be quite overbearing with our son.*

re|served ADJ Someone who is **reserved** keeps their feelings hidden. • *He was unemotional, quite quiet, and reserved.*

threat|en|ing ADJ You can describe someone's behaviour as **threatening** when you think that they are trying to harm you.

wary ADJ If you are **wary of** something or someone, you are cautious because you do not know much about them and you believe they may be dangerous or cause problems. • *They were very wary about giving him a contract.*

Unit 20

ban VERB To **ban** something means to state officially that it must not be done, shown, or used. • *He was banned from driving for three years.*

clut|ter N-UNCOUNT **Clutter** is a lot of things in an untidy state, especially things that are not useful or necessary. • *I prefer my worktops to be clear of clutter.*

frown upon or **frown on** If something **is frowned upon** or **is frowned on** people disapprove of it. • *This practice is frowned upon as being wasteful.*

ice-breaker also **icebreaker** N-COUNT An **ice-breaker** is something that someone says or does in order to make it easier for people who have never met before to talk to each other. • *This exercise can be quite a useful ice-breaker for new groups.*

spick and span also **spick-and-span** ADJ A place that is **spick and span** is very clean and tidy. • *The apartment was spick and span.*

stag|ger VERB To **stagger** things such as people's holidays or hours of work means to arrange them so that they do not all happen at the same time. • *During the past few years the government has staggered the summer vacation periods for students.*

ANSWER KEY

Unit 1

A
1

1 His rising intonation.
2 His use of 'r' and strong, round vowels.
3 He has slowed down his speed of delivery.
4 About three hours.

3

1 anything
2 mellowed
3 rising
4 'R'
5 vowels
6 the speed of delivery
7 anglicised [anglicized in US English]
8 reverts

4

1c 2f 3a 4b 5d 6e

B
1

1 To be clear.
2 He will use incorrect grammar if necessary to get his message across.
3 Having the ability to communicate clearly.
4 The importance of slowing down (in order to be understood).

2

1 few months
2 amending or adapting
3 complex clauses
4 get the message
5 I'm speaking
6 critical part
7 business obstacle
8 slowing down

C
1

1 Writing emails to customers who are based internationally.
2 Communicating in French with French customers.
3 She needs to bear in mind that she should use 'standard' language and avoid idioms and colloquialisms.
4 Because they talked so quickly and often used acronyms.

2

1 point of view
2 with great respect
3 essentially
4 Indian expats
5 48%
6 encourage

Unit 2

A
1

1 They speak very quickly.
2 The Philippines.
3 She feels that Nigerian speakers talk quickly and they speak with different intonation and different accents on syllables.
4 She feels 'blurry' and her mind is spinning. (Possibly her Nigerian colleagues feel the same!)

3

1 repeatedly
2 repeating

3 gotten
4 used to
5 accented
6 blurry by the end of it

B
1

1 25
2 Culture and region.
3 Sometimes it's possible to tell, but it depends on whether they actually have a regional accent, and how strong it is.
4 It is not easy as she does not have a regional accent.

3

1 each value is printed
2 vary
3 make out
4 regional
5 break into
6 other than

C

1

1 When he deals with people who don't normally speak English.

2 Grammar and unfamiliar (or incorrect) terms and words.
3 To read between the lines.

2

1 native English
2 Denmark or you work with a French
3 normally
4 tend to have to
5 aspect

Unit 3

A

1

1 The hash or pound key (#).
2 No – the system does not recognise the pass code she enters.
3 Press star followed by zero.
4 Four people (three, and then Nigel joins late).
5 Lorna says it's very cold and very crispy.

2

1 please enter
2 invalid
3 has been confirmed
4 activates
5 makes up
6 minus one (-1°C)

B

1

1 Wednesday (tomorrow).
2 The hold-up with some outstanding invoices.

3 He said that he thought that they had everything they needed for the hand-over.
4 They sent back an email highlighting what information is missing.
5 She is going to look in her inbox to check if she was copied in to the email (cc'd) or whether the email was forwarded to her.

2

3 1 6 2 5 8 4 7

3

1 queries
2 outstanding
3 under the impression
4 highlighting
5 double-check
6 forwarded that on
7 the case

4

1b 2d 3a 4c 5f 6e

Unit 4

A

1

1 The meeting scheduled for next Thursday at 3 o'clock.
2 The meeting clashes with another meeting on the other side of town.
3 She will need to reschedule it.
4 Between 4 and 4.30.

2

1 calling
2 just
3 Unfortunately
4 have to
5 a call
6 appreciate

3

1 3 o'clock.
2 Sitting in a traffic jam on the M25.
3 He still has a one hour journey ahead of him.
4 30 minutes ('half an hour').

4

1 Terribly
2 appointment
3 currently
4 mobile number
5 a call

B

1

1 True
2 False – she says 'if you are staying in …' which suggests that she does not know.
3 True
4 False – she mentions a taxi and other means of transport as possible ways of travelling from Tiananmen station to the hotel, but she does not strongly recommend any one option.

3

1 She is very busy at the moment.
2 Take a taxi or a bus.
3 At the station entrance.

4

5 3 8 2 6 4 1 7

C

1

1 Walk to the main road.
2 She forgets the name of the station (but then, after she thinks for a moment, she remembers it).
3 Number 82.
4 A taxi.

2

1 pick you up
2 take
3 company
4 drive
5 difficult

Unit 5

A

1

1 Bentonville, Arkansas.
2 It was a shock in terms of how low-key and relaxed the atmosphere was. He was surprised at how rural the setting was.
3 Seattle.
4 It is very much 'work hard, play hard'.

3

1 rural
2 purpose-built
3 weight
4 disarming
5 having gone

4

I think
you know
basically
I have to say
it's like
sort of
you probably

B

1

1 In the city.
2 It is much faster in the city – more 'hustle and bustle'.
3 In the city.

C

1

1 It is very different.
2 Canadians are proud of their links.
3 In Catrina's view, Canadians are more relaxed. She thinks that Americans tend to be workaholics.

2

1 so fluid
2 don't even realise
3 different to
4 quite proud
5 deeply embroiled
6 friendlier
7 more laid-back
8 tend to be

3

Relaxed
laid back
calm
tranquil
quiet
peaceful

Not relaxed
go-go-go
frenetic
hectic
chaotic
demanding
frantic
busy

Unit 6

A

1

1   You should socialise with and get to know
    prospective business partners before you do business
    with them.
2   They have thought that going for lunch would be
    more appropriate after doing a business deal, not
    before.
3   He believes they would be 'taken aback' – a little
    shocked.

2

1   relationships
2   your friends
3   really reluctant
4   long, long phase
5   quite alien
6   initiate business
7   business is finished

B

1

1   No, he doesn't.
2   In Owen's opinion, not at all. It is strict.
3   Yes, very expensive.
4   It makes it very difficult to set up small businesses
    and inhibits their growth.

3

1   (very) straightforward
2   non-existent
3   extraordinarily
4   flexible
5   strict
6   astronomical
7   inhibit
8   stability

4

1b   2d   3f   4a   5c   6h   7e   8g

C

1

1   They eat first.
2   Peru.
3   Germany.

2

1   work
2   eat
3   treat
4   the contrary
5   easier
6   circle
7   get

Unit 7

A

1

1   A big multicultural, diverse society with extremes of
    terrain, and climate and wealth.
2   They have created job opportunities, allowing Indians
    to remain in their homeland and still use their talents.
3   Indian people work hard and play hard.

2

1   True
2   True

3   False – this used to be true but is no longer the case.
4   False – they have a 'work hard, play hard' mentality.

4

1   sides to it
2   poorest
3   rural
4   of course, emerging
5   the multinationals
6   as opposed to
7   weren't being
8   hang out

B

1 Two weeks.
2 No, just slight cultural differences.
3 Understanding accents and regional differences.

2

1 back-to-back
2 in terms
3 perception
4 given that
5 engage
6 accents or regional

Unit 8

A

1

1 Materials are cheap and wages are low. They want to buy things in China.
2 He says they are treated like gods. They are customers and that is how customers are treated in China.
3 They are left to look after themselves and have to buy their own transport and make their own accommodation arrangements.
4 It is important to form good relationships if you are to do business in China. You must become friends, and good friends are not arrogant.

3

1 cheaper
2 used to
3 very scheduled

4 waste time
5 competitor

B

1

1 They prioritise good business relationships.
2 They should have dinner together.
3 You should drink together and initiate a toast.
4 In northern China.

3

1 practice
2 challenging
3 Basically
4 rapport
5 liquor
6 initiate

Unit 9

A

1

1 To get directions from the airport.
2 Next week.
3 A taxi.
4 About 2 dollars.
5 25 dollars.

2

1 a taxi rank
2 save the cash
3 roughly
4 take you
5 to make
6 worries

B

1

1 To let him know that he is landing in Rio next Thursday and to confirm their 2 p.m. meeting.
2 The meeting time is no longer convenient for Bernardo as his colleague cannot attend the meeting at that time.
3 He has a hospital appointment.
4 Friday afternoon at 2 p.m.

2

1 just wanted
2 it was
3 glad you called
4 who was supposed to
5 suggest
6 actually going to be / actually gonna be

C

1

1 Next Thursday.
2 He will still be travelling at that time.
3 She already has an all-day meeting scheduled.
4 Tuesday (the following week) at 1 p.m.
5 At Celia's offices.

2

1 in the diary
2 do the Friday / reschedule
3 following

4 check my calendar
5 just to reconfirm
6 flexible

3

It's great to hear from you.
No problem.
Monday is not great for me.
Friday's not so good for me, I'm afraid.
Sorry about that.
When would suit?
Does that work for you?
Is that any good?

Unit 10

A

1

1 To drink with them.
2 They have a formal relationship.
3 Chisato says that Japanese people do not show their real character and express their true opinions.

3

1 formal
2 together
3 relationship
4 different way
5 real opinion
6 mood

B

1

1 Occasionally.
2 To a nice dinner (not at home), to a play, a game of football or something similar.
3 The 'tailgate' is the rear end of a pick-up truck where you can load things or sit.
4 Typically before a football game.

2

1 client to lunch
2 prospective clients
3 very much
4 imagine
5 meeting up

3

Suggested answers – some dishes can be eaten in a variety of ways

1 Main dishes: chicken legs, ribs, steak sandwich, hot dogs, burgers
2 Side dishes: stuffed peppers, baked beans, coleslaw, potato salad, olives, chips
3 Dips/toppings: pickles, relish, guacamole, salsa, ketchup
4 Food preparation: grill, cooler, ice, drinks, plates, silverware

4

1 baseball
2 picnic
3 skidoo
4 polo
5 karaoke
6 shashlik
7 fondue
8 cricket

Unit 11

A

1

1 Peking duck.
2 The duck is roasted with the skin on so that the skin remains crispy and the meat is tender.

3 You put the duck meat into a type of taco with some sauce. [The 'type of taco' that Yue tries to describe is usually described in English as being 'like a pancake'.]
4 The sauce is sweet and a little salty – it tastes delicious.

3

1 gristly
2 tasty
3 tender
4 poached
5 vegetarian
6 lean
7 live
8 delicacy

B
1

1 Her Mum's home cooking.
2 'Quite rarely' – not very often.
3 Before she went to Japan, Nikki thought that Japanese people ate sushi frequently.
4 A supermarket, or a convenience store such as 7-Eleven.
5 Lots of rice, with something on the rice. Lots of meat, and some sushi.
6 Raw chicken liver.

2

1 miss

2 sushi
3 pile of
4 roll
5 lunchbox
6 get it all

3

1b 2a 3f 4g 5d 6e 7c

C
1

1 His familiar food and his community.
2 Home cooking (from his country).
3 Three to six months.

3

1 ibbeh
2 baba ghanoush
3 shawarma
4 hummus
5 falafel
6 baklava
7 tabouleh
8 pitta bread

Unit 12

A
1

1 Because he could drive to Clapham and then take the tube (underground) from there.
2 No.
3 Because he likes living in the countryside.
4 17 and almost 15 years old.
5 Twenty minutes by car from the south coast of England.

2

1 yellow lines
2 so far out
3 of getting
4 a tube
5 make the odd
6 put up with
7 hassle
8 more difficult
9 tricky
10 daily grind

3

1c 2e 3a 4b 5f 6d

4

But hey

So …
I just …
I think that's …
You know, …
As I say, …

B
1

1 No, not as willing as she is.
2 Yes, very strong.
3 It is not good for family life.

2

1 appreciate
2 less willing
3 strong work ethic
4 our demise
5 for Mom or Dad
6 positive change

3

1 determined   motivated
2 ambitious
3 strong-minded
4 positive   decisive
5 keen
6 tenacious   persistent

Unit 13

A

1

1 Once a month – the third Monday of every month.
2 HR and IT inductions.
3 She takes the new employees for a walk and explains the layout of the office and makes sure that they know where the key places are.
4 The nearest fire exit.
5 She tells them what they can expect to find there and tells them about the canteen opening hours.

3

1 attending
2 meet them
3 building
4 nearest
5 canteen
6 post

4

1c 2a 3f 4e 5d 6b 7h 8g

B

1

1 True
2 True
3 False – she says that it was very exciting, and there was always something dramatic happening.
4 False – the 24-hour drama meant that it wasn't something that she would want to do long-term.
5 True

2

1 got involved
2 landed
3 blood pumping
4 back-stabbing / affairs
5 burn-out
6 morals / ethical
7 roll your sleeves
8 ethic

3

1c 2a 3e 4g 5f 6h 7b 8d

Unit 14

A

1

1 The Chartered Institute of Management Accountancy.
2 Balance sheets and P&Ls (profit and loss accounts).
3 Management accountants are more 'internally focused' on the company whereas financial accountants are more 'outwardly focused'.

3

1 qualified
2 financial
3 auditor
4 shareholders
5 division
6 outcome
7 other than

4

1 ledgers
2 cash flow
3 shareholder
4 assets
5 currencies
6 Interest

B

1

1 No, they work in a different city.
2 'Putting the accruals', looking after the general ledger. [Liz explains what she meant by this: 'Maintaining the financial accounts to ensure the records are fair and true, and are of an auditable standard. This can include balance sheet reconciliations, allocating costs and revenues to General Ledger accounts and investigating any anomalies.']
3 No. He also has various other tasks beyond his role of overseeing the management accountancy team. Liz mentions that he looks after people who are purchasing currency, people who do the transactions and also the call centre operations (where customers make orders).

2

1 team
2 division / purchase
3 balance
4 P&L
5 nitty-gritty
6 purchasing

C

1

1 False – Tonya says her company employs 'less than a hundred people'.
2 True
3 False – she has been with her current company for over 3 years, so she left the Fortune 500 company some time before that.
4 True

2

1 public
2 firm
3 reviewing
4 ensuring / complying
5 good bit
6 training
7 Prior
8 internal

Unit 15

A

1

1 12 months.
2 90% of your salary for six weeks.
3 Yes (or an equivalent role) – but this is only true if you return within the first twelve months.
4 Two weeks at 90% of full pay, and it can usually be taken at any time – not necessarily at the time of the birth.
5 Three or four weeks.

3

1 due
2 cover
3 disruption
4 entitled
5 sacrifice
6 notice
7 statutory
8 birth

B

1

1 Nine and eleven years old.
2 Two days plus an unspecified amount of annual leave.
3 No, he doesn't.
4 No, he wouldn't.

3

1 weren't gifted
2 ordinary annual
3 equal treatment
4 personal circumstances
5 adequate
6 part of our plan

C

1

1 No, it wasn't a total surprise (but it was still a shock).
2 Her boss's boss.
3 Her company was being taken over by another company.
4 She got it as a result of extensive networking.
5 She was headhunted for it.

2

1 made redundant
2 happened
3 was planning on
4 boss's boss
5 was formalised
6 got in touch
7 freelance contract
8 was headhunted

Unit 16

A

1

1 Good preparation and planning.
2 It was to make the trip as meaningful as possible, to cut down on travelling time and to speed up the assessment of prospective suppliers and partners.
3 She coordinated the main schedules for the supplier visits.
4 The suppliers had moved premises and had not informed anyone.
5 The phone numbers were out of date.
6 Two hours outside the city of Chennai.

2

1 teed
2 prospective
3 technical packs
4 pulled
5 dozens
6 premises
7 irrelevant
8 turned out
9 reschedule

3

Possible answers

1 reschedule
2 coordinate (*or* pull together)
3 attend
4 turn out
5 line up (*or* prepare, coordinate, reschedule)
6 pull together (*or* coordinate)
7 prepare
8 assist

4

1c 2a 3g 4b 5f 6e 7h 8d

B

1

1 From Sunday to Thursday.
2 She had to be aware of cultural sensitivities.
3 About a week.
4 10 days.

2

1 dealing
2 consideration
3 accordingly
4 sensitivities
5 adapt
6 tag on
7 nip

Unit 17

A

1

1 When people 'insist their opinion' = when people insist that they are right, when they are overly opinionated.
2 Chisato says that Confucianism dictates that one should obey one's elders.
3 They feel uncomfortable.

3

Suggested answers

1 The boss orders some work from Westerners. *or* The boss asks Westerners to do a particular job/task.
2 The boss is often/usually much older. *or* The boss will usually be much older.
3 Sometimes Westerners insist that they are right. *or* Sometimes Westerners are highly opinionated.
4 So I guess it is difficult / it can be difficult for Japanese people to adjust to Western people.

B

1

1 False – Frederic says that the French like to discuss things and to challenge one another during negotiations.
2 True
3 True

2

1 is conducted
2 making a
3 perceived / intrusive
4 rather than

3

Suggested answers

1 People that like to argue …
2 If someone cares about what you're doing …
3 If someone cares about your opinion …
   or If someone is interested in your opinion …
4 He will probably challenge you and ask you a lot of questions.

4

Positive features	Negative features
dynamic	intrusive
perceptive	interfering
energetic	insensitive
purposeful	clumsy
courteous	discourteous

C

1

1 She is a legal consultant in a large company.
2 Different companies in the US and UK as well as some local companies.

3   In her opinion, the Japanese are meticulous (they focus on every detail) whereas the Chinese are not.
4   They believe in getting things done as quickly as possible.

2

1   to negotiate
2   to confirm
3   market[ing] department
4   be pushed
5   emphasise
6   finish this project

3

Suggested answers

1   They focus on every word.
2   They (will) need confirmation from their Head Office or Legal Department / legal advisor / legal consultant.
3   So it's quite long.
    or So it can take a long time.
4   Maybe some companies don't concern themselves with the legal side of things too much.
    or Perhaps some companies are not so concerned about legalities
5   They prefer to finish a project as soon as possible.

Unit 18

A
1

1   No.
2   No.
3   No.
4   It is strange (and inappropriate in the west).

2

1   based
2   tolerance
3   literal meaning
4   getting at
5   signed it
6   kind of

B
1

1   By email or telephone.
2   Germany.
3   Use email instead of speaking on the phone.
4   A dictionary.

2

1   misunderstanding[s]
2   Germany [Jing says 'German']
3   native speaker

4   understand
5   write down
6   find out

C
1

1   Roughly once a month.
2   No.
3   Telephone, email and instant messaging.
4   It solidifies a partnership and cements relationships. It also creates a good impression from the customer's point of view.

2

1   is based
2   constraints
3   up and down
4   keep up
5   are willing
6   every so often
7   solidifies

3

1   once
2   every
3   in
4   until
5   by
6   on
7   since
8   weekly

Unit 19

A
1

1   A friend, or a friend of a friend.
2   No.
3   The mix of nationalities in London. It is a very multicultural city.
4   She thinks hugging is maybe most appropriate when you know the people, and after a certain length of time.

2

1   you could kiss
2   not going to / gonna
3   are shocked
4   touching someone
5   both cheeks
6   hugging

3

'Appropriate' behaviour

respectful   easy-going
reassuring   polite
warm   supportive
welcoming   professional

'Inappropriate' behaviour

threatening   impolite
insulting   cold
overbearing   hostile
rude   offensive

B

1

1 Yes, they are. They enjoy being together.
2 From the south of the country.
3 He hugs them and kisses them on the cheek.
4 Yes.
5 His normal behaviour would be to kiss male and female friends but he thinks that, in the UK, some people may query his sexuality if he kisses male friends when he greets them.

3

1 easy-going
2 used to
3 hug and to kiss
4 hide
5 express myself

C

1

1 False – she says most of her colleagues are women.
2 True
3 True
4 False – the opposite is true. You should always hand over a business card with two hands.

2

1 colleagues
2 not supposed to
3 tend to be
4 nuances
5 hand over

Unit 20

A

1

1 False – it depends on the kind of business.
2 False – she would prefer to work straight through the day.
3 True
4 True

3

1c   2a   3b   4f   5d   6e

B

1

1 Spanish, Polish and German.
2 A quiet, clean and tidy world – a 'heavenly' world.
3 People chatting, walking around, making a noise – a 'hellish' world.
4 He is half Italian, half Colombian.
5 Because they hide their emotions.
6 Happiness or excitement.

2

1 shared
2 Dante's 'Hells' = Dante's Hell
3 productive
4 smiling
5 sad

6 sound
7 were behaving in

3

Organised	Disorganised
uncluttered	cluttered
neat	chaotic
calm	muddled
ordered	messy

C

1

1 4 hours.
2 4 p.m.
3 From 8 a.m. till 5.15 p.m.
4 Around 7 a.m.
5 They have to clean up and make sure everything is tidy.

2

1 part-time
2 seven o'clock
3 picks up
4 five-fifteen
5 until about
6 spick-and-span

TRANSCRIPTS

The transcripts below are an exact representation of what each speaker on the *Listening* CD says. No corrections or adaptations have been made.

Unit 1   Communicating clearly

Track 1

Certainly, thirty years after leaving Northern Ireland I— I would never…uh…accept that I'm anything except Northern Irish. I think the accent has mellowed, I mean the— the intonation has probably not changed very much. Um…I speak with quite a rising intonation, which has actually caused some problems with people who, at the end of a telephone conversation, when I've said, 'OK, well I'll talk to you later', thought that I was asking another question and paused. So I'd try and say goodbye and they— they'd say, 'What did you ask?' And this is really something very specific to do with the— the— the nature of my local English accent from Northern Ireland. It's very typical. There's a joke in my home town that you don't need a road map to get around – you need the score.

People say I speak very clearly and I think it's because, you know, like Americans we have an 'R'. We don't drop the 'R' as in— in Received Pronunciation. And also I think the vowels are quite round and— and quite strong. And I think, over the years, I've actually modified the way I speak. I've slowed the speed of delivery down quite considerably. Um…But when I go back home, people say I've become extremely anglicised, and after about three hours it speeds up again and it goes back to— sort of reverts to type. So there— there's— there's— there's definitely a— a— a…period after which I become much more…uh…strong in the way that I pronounce words.

Track 2

I decided…uh…after my first few months working in…uh…the export market that the first and most important thing I had to do was to be clear – and if that meant amending and— or adapting the way that I speak to make it easier for people to understand me, then that's what I would do. And I also find that I avoid more complex…um…clauses in— in sentences. I actually have— have a second, simpler language that I try and speak. I would leave out subjunctive clauses and subordinate clauses and…I shouldn't say it but I occasionally will speak incorrect grammar just to get the message across – put the word— change the word order slightly so that people can follow the track – depending— depending on, of course, the language skills of the person I'm speaking to. But I think that's the most critical part of the job. I think it's more important than the— the— the knowledge of the business or the product knowledge. I think if you can't let people understand you easily, you're already up against a— a business obstacle. So slowing down is by far the most important thing that I learnt in the first year.

Track 3

Writing emails to customers who are based…uh…internationally…uh…was— was a challenge from time to time but I guess from my point of view…um…I just had to explain things as clearly as possible and just remember, with great respect, that…um…these people are writing to me in a language that is not their native…uh…language, which—

which for me is— is— is amazing. Um…I mean, I've worked with French customers so I'd occasionally…um…I'd have the shoe on the other foot and…uh…have to communicate in French which, you know, took a long time and…and it was— it was hard to communicate in— in another language. But essentially working internationally is just sort of bearing in mind that you just have to use quite standard language and avoid, sort of, idioms and colloquialisms.

Well, when I worked with customers in the UAE there were lots of…um…Indian expats living in the UAE. In fact, 48% of the population…um…was Indian…um…in— in that— in that area and…um…occasionally I'd find…uh…that my Indian customers would talk very, very quickly and…um…often use acronyms…um…which I'd— I'd have to…encourage them to explain!

Unit 2   Understanding different accents

Track 4

Some of the accents, as a native English speaker, I still find quite difficult – especially when…um…they— in their mind, they speak English fluently so they will speak very quickly. Uh…and it's— it's extremely hard to— to get every word and…uh…I feel very rude in meetings sometimes repeatedly saying, 'Excuse me?' 'Pardon me?' 'Would you mind repeating that?' Um…but my ear has gotten better at the various accents throughout the years. Uh…Especially with…um…The easiest market is the Philippines 'cos they— they all speak…um…and— and read in English. Um…They only have…um…about two or three shelves in each bookstore of their own native language, Tagalog. So…um…that's the best one to visit in terms of minimal headaches in meetings.

I used to work with a lot of Nigerian customers in my old position in New York and…th— they speak English. That's their official language, but it's such a quick…um…accented English and…uh…with…just…different intonations and different accents on— on syllables…uh…that— after a full day of meetings you feel so blurry by the end of it. Your…just…mind is spinning. So I can't imagine, if someone from France is speaking in English to someone from Nigeria speaking in English, how they would be able to communicate with each other. I mean obviously they do, but…I think it would be more difficult.

Track 5

India's a very diverse land of many different cultures and languages and dialects and…We have about twenty-five different languages – official languages. So our currency— on our currency, each value is printed twenty-four times in a— in each official language. That's the rule. So…um…yes. A— and yes, of course, according—…uh…based on the culture and based on different regions, the accents vary as well. So…North Indians have a different accent, the people from Punjab have a different accent, people from Kashmir have a very different accent and people in the south have a diff— have different accents – so it's very, very diverse. Sometimes you can make out if an Indian is from a certain region but it really depends on whether they have that regional accent or not, because you can lose the regional accent and sometimes you don't – especially when they speak English. It depends on how strong their regional accent is. Uh…I— my— I don't have a regional accent so nobody would be able to tell where I'm from. I might break into my regional accent if I were to come across somebody from my region but other than that, no.

Track 6

I mean, lot of us in India are native English speakers. We tend to— tend to speak English ...uh...you know, as...uh...in our day-to-day lives. But...uh...if you work with somebody in Denmark or you work with a French guy, you know, you— you have...people who don't normally speak English also conducting business in English. And I think that's when it gets a little more difficult because...uh...now you— you have...uh...not only...uh...accent to— to take care of but you also have sometimes...uh...grammar and, you know, ...uh...t— terms and words that are not ac— not actually what— what they meant to say, but you— you tend to have to, you know, read— read between the lines. And that's— that's the other aspect of...uh...of working globally in English.

Unit 3   Conference calls

Track 7

Conference voice	At any time during this message, please enter your participant pass code followed by the hash or pound sign now.
	The pass code you are attempting to enter – three, three, eight, three, eight, three, five, two – is invalid. Please re-enter your participant pass code followed by the hash or pound sign now.
	Thank you. Your pass code has been confirmed.
	If you are a participant, you may hear music until the leader activates the conference. If you need technical assistance during your call, please press star followed by zero. If you are the leader, please press the star key now.
	After the tone, please state your name, followed by the hash or pound sign.
	[beep]
	I'm sorry; we did not get your name. After the tone, please state your name followed, by the hash or pound sign.
	[beep]
Lorna	Lorna
Conference voice	The leader has not activated this conference; please stand by until your call begins.
	[music]
	There are three parties in the conference including you.
Lorna	Hello?
Edmund	Hello, Edmund here.
Lorna	Hi, Edmund.
Alex	Hi, Edmund.
Lorna	Hi, Alex.
Edmund	Hi, guys.
Alex	Hello, Lorna.
Lorna	Hi. Is Nigel on?...Not yet, then! How is everyone? Good weekend?
Edmund	Yes, thank you.
Alex	Yes, very pleasant, thanks. How about you?

Lorna	Yeah, yeah, same. Um…I think…uh…we had a couple of…um…uh…I was gonna say rain-free days, but actually I think we had a couple of hours without showers, really. That would kind of sum it up, really.
Edmund	It's— it's a lovely day down here today. Uh…Makes up for yesterday, really.
Lorna	Yeah…um…one of the ladies here was saying minus five when she got up…uh…this morning. And it was— Certainly it was minus one by the time I'd got out to the car today. But it's very cold, very crispy up here today; very lovely!
Nigel	Hello, this is Nigel.
Lorna	Hi, Nigel, how are you?
Nigel	Hi, Lorna.
Lorna	Right, we've got Alex and we've got Edmund in the call now.
Nigel	Hi guys.
Lorna	OK, then. Edmund, do you want to take us through your highlight report, please?

Track 8

Anna	And if you've got any queries in the meantime with any of those, please let me know. Alex has been on holiday for the past two weeks but he's back on Wednesday – tomorrow. Um…So we know that there's a couple of outstanding invoices…um…which — I'll get him to double-check…um…what the hold-up is there…um…and we'll get that then processed. And they should be processed already so I'll just che— I'll check with Finance to see what the hold-up is there.
Rohit	OK, sure.
Anna	OK?
Rohit	Uh…Anna, another question…uh…was regarding the…s— ation [*bad line*]…why that's still not resolved, so what is the status on that?
Anna	Well, I spoke to Bill and he said that he thought that we had everything we needed to hand it over. So it would be useful if you could compose an email…uh…which I could forward on, which just outlines what's missing or what's still outstanding 'cos he's under the impression that they've forwarded everything on that you need.
Rohit	I think I sent that…uh…to— to Alex quite— quite a long time ago so I don't know if…uh…it's—
Eddie	We just…uh…sent back an email highlighting what is missing— what information is missing, and…uh…it's been almost a month.
Anna	Um…I'll have a— I'll look for that— If I have a look for that in my inbox, I may have been cc'd or forwarded. If I forward— bounce that back to you, and if you could just check that that's still the case, and then I'll— I'll forward it on to Bill. Um…Let me just— In fact, I may have that just now. Um…I'll double check…um…I'll double check if I've still got that email. I think I forwarded that on to Bill with a view to— that that was still outstanding. But…um…let me just double-check that and if I just forward it onto you again, you can confirm that that's still the case. Then we can chase up just to get that handed over once and for all.
Rohit	Yes, no problem.
Anna	Okay?
Eddie	All right, Anna.

Anna	That's super. Thank you for that.
Rohit	Nice talking to you, Anna.
Anna	And you. Thank you very much.
Eddie	You're welcome. Bye bye.
Rohit	Bye bye.
Anna	Bye now.

Unit 4   Voicemails

Track 9

Hi, Marie. It's Catrina calling. Uh…I'm just calling about the meeting we have scheduled for next Thursday at three o'clock. Unfortunately, I have another meeting that's come into my schedule…um…that's on the other side of town, so I'm gonna have to reschedule for another time. I hope you're free around four, four-thirty. If you could give me a call back, I'd really appreciate it. Thanks very much. Bye.

Track 10

Oh hi, it's Nick. Um…Terribly sorry, I— I know we've got an appointment at three o'clock but I'm currently sat on the M25 doing no miles an hour and it's half past two so I've got about an hour to— to run to get to you so I'm gonna be about half an hour late. Um…You know my mobile number so give me a call if you need to talk to me.

Track 11

If you want to get from the— from the airport to the downtown, you can take the Airport Express. There are a lot— are a lot of lines and…uh…maybe one line will— will go to Xidan and one line will go to…uh…Chaoyang and— and a lot— and a lot of place. So…um…if your hotel is in Tiananmen, you can take the lines— you can take the lines between the airport to Xidan and you can get down— get down when the bus came to the Tiananmen station. And you can go to your hotel by taxi or by— by bus, by subway.

Track 12

Hello, Peter. I'm so sorry that I can't meet you since I'm so busy now. And you can take a taxi or a bus to the Heshui Road which is the station next to the Xigu District. Uh…Maybe…uh…when you get here and the— in the entrance, I will meet you there.

Track 13

Hello, Paul. I'm sorry I cannot pick you up today but you can go and meet me at the company. You just easily by walk to the main road and catch the…um…Skytrain, yeah. Then you buy the ticket to the…oh, I forgot the place…to the Phayathai Junction, and then you take off and then you may take the bus if you want to – the bus number 82. Just tell them the company name and they would know. But if you prefer the taxi, you can catch the taxi – any taxi – and then just tell them the name of the company and they will drive you there. It's not too difficult.

Unit 5   USA and Canada

Track 14

We do a lot of business with Walmart and they're based in Bentonville, Arkansas, which is the town— a little rural town in Arkansas which was where Sam Walton had his first corner shop. And they— they've built up— The single biggest retailer in the world is based out of what is a Podunk, quite rural little town. And having come from—Uh…I think I— on my last business trip there, I came straight from Manhattan into, you know, the— an airport that's purpose-built by Walmart for the town, for people – basically reps, sales people – to fly into. And…um…I have to say, you know, it's such a— You go from skyscrapers to…I wouldn't call it prairie but, you know…um…sort of Arkansas scrub. Um…It's a real shock to the system, even— And you probably don't necessarily give them the same sort of…uh…oh gosh, weight, stance, attitude as you would if you were dealing with somebody— if they were headquartered in Manhattan, you know? I think I probably would have been smartened up a bit. It was…um…relaxing, disarming, and probably works to their favour more than it did mine. But…uh…that's just— I think that was a recent real sort of shock to the system going from— That trip was New York; Bentonville, Arkansas; Birmingham, Alabama; Sea—…uh…San Diego, where, you know, suddenly having gone from winter-summer, then I went back for the winter in Seattle and then home. Um…it was…uh…interesting to see the different lifestyle things going on, how an office life— how office life works in a very different— different way. It's very much 'work hard, play hard' in Manhattan, it's 'family' in Birmingham and…uh…and Bentonville. San Diego just seemed to be about getting outside…um…and— and Seattle was— we drank a lot of coffee!

Track 15

I think there are differences in work ethic and culture obviously across the different regions in the United States. Like New York City may have more— a little more of a stronger work ethic as a result of the 'go-go-go' mentality of living in the city, as compared to someone who grew up on a farm. Now we don't have very many farms left, but they're out there. A farm requires a great deal of work but someone who is not in— has not grown up in the metropolitan area, they generally have a slower pace. They still get all the work done – just at a little slower pace.

Now, I'm in Atlanta, Georgia. Now, it's a metropolitan area, hustling and bustling. Um…It's really very different and I have to tell you, I prefer the hustle and bustle!

Track 16

I'd say the US and Canada are quite similar. I mean, the…um…just popular culture…um…is so fluid between the two countries. Um…I mean, half of the biggest Canadian stars most people don't even realise are Canadian. They just assume that they're American. Um…But of course, the Canadian heritage is— is quite different to— to the American heritage. Um…I think Canadians are quite proud of their link to England…um…and British culture, and, you know, that— all of that history is quite deeply embroiled in— in being Canadian. Um…And you know it's a— it's a friendlier nation. Not to put Americans down by any stretch but…um…it's a— it's a much more laid-back, quieter kind of way of life. Um…And Canadians typically…um…typically are much friendlier and a little less 'workaholicky' than Americans are. Americans tend to be quite 'go-go-go'.

Unit 6   Ireland and Germany

Track 17

Irish culture's mostly about relationships. It's— it's a lot about … um … you know, who you know, who your friends are. Um … And even in bu— in business terms, you'll find a lot of Irish people are really reluctant to do business with people who— they haven't, you know, gone drinking with them or seen them socially or something like that. So there's— there's this long, long phase of, like, getting to know potential customers and things like that in Irish business terms … um … which— which is quite alien to … um … to people here. I mean, I— I've often done it when trying to initiate business with a new client – like, immediately trying to bring them out for lunch and they're totally taken aback by it. They're like, 'No, that's something we do when business is finished, not before we begin.' But … um … if some— someone visiting Ireland, they'd probably be taken aback by how overly familiar people are straight away. They tend to …

Track 18

Oh well, it's chalk and cheese. I mean, in Ireland people are very … uh … How shall I say it? It— It's a— it's— it's 'jobs for the boys' culture. It's … um … You have contacts, you have friends, oh, they'll do you a favour, you'll do them a favour. Um … Business in Germany is very— very straightforward and very— in one way, strict. People are very— There's a hierarchical system in Germany that simply doesn't exist in Ireland. Um … And also I think in Ireland the laws are— Laws … uh …, in doing business, are almost non-existent. So hiring people is very easy, firing people is very easy. Uh … Setting up small businesses is extraordinarily easy. Um … it's very flexible and— and it's very liberal. There are— The government tends to let businesses go and do what they want. Um … And, of course, it's the exact opposite in Germany. It's extraordinarily strict and difficult to do anything. And the economic costs of hiring someone as a full-time employee are ' yeah ' astronomical. The difficulties of setting up businesses are— really, really inhibit the growth of small business. Um … On the other hand, there's far more, then, control and stability here in Germany.

Track 19

Yeah, in— in Peru is very informal work, and you— for example, if you wanna talk about business, you go eat. You eat first and then you talk about business. And I think here it's more like you just talk about business or you go— you talk— you go eat, you talk about business, then you eat or something like that. It's … uh … yeah, it's— it's quite — quite different.

Is like in German— in Germany it's more— it's— it's colder … um … the way the people treat each other. Peru is much, much … uh … warmer. And that's— would be good there, and bad here. But on the contrary, in Peru, you … uh … you— it's just very, very hard to— to— to get something. Uh … On the contrary, here it's— it's— it's easier just to— to make business. I think it goes straight. And in Peru is more like you make, like, circles and much difficult, and in the end you don't get that— what you want, what you need.

Unit 7   India

Track 20

I think if somebody were going to India I— I would like them to see India the way it is. India is what it is. It's a— it's a big … um … you know, it's— it's a big, multicultural, diverse society and they should see it the way it is. Uh, I don't— I think that … um … that India has different sides to it, just like India has different terrains. We have from the most barren to the most lush terrain, and similar climates: we have the most extreme cold to the most extreme warm. And it's with the people as well and with the culture as well. And we have the poorest and we also have the— the wealthy. We have the corporate and we have the rural. And I think that's— that's the impression that people get and that's the impression they're going to get when they go there.

The— The corporate is, of course, emerging in the world and, you know, really making— making a— making a name for itself and— and that's … I think that's well deserved because people have worked very, very hard since the multi-nationals have come in. Uh … It's made a huge difference – they've created job opportunities and our talent, for a change, is staying in India as opposed to having to look overseas for opportunities. Nobody really wants to— Most people don't really want to leave their home country but people have had to for— for a— We had this period where— because they felt— where people left the country because they felt that their talents weren't being used— utilised enough, or they weren't being rewarded enough. But all that is changing now and … uh … the working culture is they work hard, they also play hard. So, you know, life doesn't stop if you finish work at nine thirty. You— you could— you can still go out and hang out with friends till midnight and come back home and it's— it's a bit crazy, but it works in India. So I think, yeah, they would— they would get— they would get … um … you know, to see different kinds of food and culture and people and, you know, smells and sights.

Track 21

Most recently, I've been in a two week business trip within India. Um … That time was spent between … um … many different … uh … Indian cities, starting Delhi, Mumbai, Chennai, Pondicherry, Bangalore. So it's quite a back-to-back trip. Um … Culturally … um … it's— it's quite different in— in India. Business relationships, however, … um … I have to say, are, you know— Most Indian companies that I've seen I've been very impressed by. Um … They're very professional in terms of how they're run. Um … Many people outside … uh … of India – many UK-based people who've perhaps never experienced business negotiations or discussions with other cultures – you know, have a perception of how these countries may … uh … may be. But, for me … um … doing business in India or China … um … is— is no different … um … really, than … um … doing business with … uh … UK colleagues. There are slight cultural differences. Um … There may be challenges in understanding accents. I include my— myself in that, given that I have a— a Scottish accent. Um … But ultimately, you know … um … there's a common … uh … language of business. Uh … And most— most of the companies that we engage with … um … are entirely professional. Uh … We're only limited in, sometimes, the understanding due to accents or— or— or regional differences.

Unit 8   China

Track 22

For foreign…uh…businessmen come to China, I think…uh…this is happened between Chinese go to abroad is that, you take money from— You— you have the— the chance for, to do business with us. But the difference is that you take money from America or Western to here. You want to buy something is cheap. Uh…Materials, or you want to establish…uh…the factory, because the worker's wage is cheaper here. So, it's different because when we go to abroad, we want to sell; you just want to buy. Then I think its— its— it's like a god, because customer is god. You are like a god to here. But when we go to abroad, it's— this makes us very cheap. No one will drive us. We just find a— a car for ourselves and buy the ticket for selves. But if you want to come China, if you wanted to have a big contract with us, then your ticket is— is for us, your— your hotel fee and your— your dinner fee is all paid by us. But for a— a foreign people to have…uh…estab— established…uh…the good relationship with a Chinese company or Chinese— Uh…Because they— many of the Chinese company and new problem I have mentioned that so they are management…uh…organisations, that there is one leader have all others follow them. So you have to…uh…. establish a good relationship with the leader. So you shouldn't be arrogant. You should be like a friend. And…uh…beside this, you shouldn't be the new bird here, because…uh…before— before you— before you go to China to have business, maybe the better way for you is to have a trip, have a— have a…uh…journey here – to western Shanghai, to western Wuhan, to know the— to— to feel the culture here, to— to let you become used to China. And then you wouldn't like a new bird.

And also you should have a very scheduled plan. You pick…uh…your— your business partners, not just one. You should list three or five of names because you don't want waste time to just…uh…come by to visit one company. And you should tell the— and you should tell the Chinese businessmen about this. Because they know that they have competitors. So the price or the…uh…relationship for you two especially will be more actively, I think.

Track 23

I think the way that people do business in China, you know— Chinese business practice is very different from Western world. Um…Like, you know, Chinese people…um…you know, it's— Talking about lots of relationship – if we know you well, then we can do a lot of things. If I don't know you well then, you know, probably, you know, things will be more challenging, some difficult. That's why you need to build a relationship or rapport. How do you do that? Basically, it's through the social, like, part— part of your social life like, you know, like— Um…Dinner is a good way for you to build the rapport because, you know, during dinner, you know, your partners – business partner – will be more relaxed. And then, you know, Chinese people like to drink— drink wine. It's Chinese liquor, not the red wine or that kind of thing. Because, you know…um…drinking the wine, you know, if you toasting each other and then you— you 'bottoms up', and it's— you're showing your respect to your partner. You know, if you initiate a toasting and then you 'bottoms up' and…um…it's really— you know, to them you feel that you— you really respect him. And then this can easily build the rapport, you know the— Particularly, this is more common for northern side of the people – North China people. They like to drink wine and then, you know, the more you drink, then the happier you guys are, you know, because then you have the guts to drink— drink with them.

Track 24

Nikki	Hi, Catrina. How you doing?
Catrina	I'm well, thanks Nikki. How are you?
Nikki	I'm very well. I'm just…um…calling you quickly to…uh…get some directions from the airport for when I come across to meet you next week.
Catrina	Oh brilliant, OK. Well…um…when you arrive, there is a taxi rank straight outside which is probably your best option in terms of getting to the— getting to the office from the airport. Um…There is a shuttle bus as well though…um…which is only about two dollars so if you— if you need to save the cash that's a— that's a good option.
Nikki	OK, but you'd recommend a taxi, would you?
Catrina	Yes, I'd definitely recommend a taxi.
Nikki	OK, and how much do you think that would cost, roughly?
Catrina	Should be about $25. You can— you can agree a flat rate once you arrive.
Nikki	Mmm hmm. And how long do you think it'll take to get to the office?
Catrina	Um … shouldn't take you more than twenty minutes.
Nikki	Right, so I should have plenty of time to make our three o'clock meeting, then.
Catrina	Oh yes! Absolutely.
Nikki	Excellent. All right, then. Thanks very much. Bye!
Catrina	No worries. Look forward to seeing you.
Nikki	You too. Bye!

Track 25

Bernardo	Hi, hello, Bernardo speaking.
John	Hi, Bernardo. It's John from the UK.
Bernardo	Hi, John. How are you?
John	I'm well. How are you?
Bernardo	I'm good, thank you.
John	Good. Um…I just wanted to…uh…let you know that I'm still landing at Rio next Thursday and wanted to confirm our meeting. Um…I think it was for 2 p.m.?
Bernardo	Ah yeah…uh…I'm glad you called, actually, 'cos…um…my colleague…uh… Rafael, who was supposed to be attending the meeting as well…Um…He's got an hospital appointment … um…so would you like to suggest any other time?
John	Right. Um…How is Friday morning for you?
Bernardo	Um…Friday morning is actually going to be difficult for me as well. Um…I've got something else on. Um…Could you say maybe Friday afternoon 2 p.m. at my office? Is that ok for you?
John	That's fine for me, thank you.
Bernardo	Oh, yeah. I guess— I guess so we are settled for Friday 2 p.m. then. And I'll see you there.
John	Great, I'll look forward to seeing you.
Bernardo	OK. Have a great…uh…journey and I'll see you in Rio.
John	Thanks very much. Bye.
Bernardo	Ok, bye bye.

Track 26

Grant	Hi, Celia. It's Grant from International Sales. How you doing?
Celia	Oh, hi, Grant. It's great to hear from you.
Grant	Um... I see that we have a meeting...um...in the diary for next Thursday.
Celia	Yes, that's right.
Grant	And...um...unfortunately I'm still gonna be on a plane at that point, coming back to...um...the UK.
Celia	Right.
Grant	Um ... Is it possible for us to reschedule at all?
Celia	Oh yes, sure...Um...No problem. Uh...When would suit?
Grant	Um...Well, I get back that Thursday afternoon, so I can either do the Friday or we—we can...um...possibly reschedule for early the following week.
Celia	Oh, OK. Um...Uh...Friday's not so good for me, I'm afraid. I've got all— an all day meeting—...um...uh...an ex— an external meeting with...um...another...um...sales—...um...sales team.
Grant	Got you.
Celia	Yes, so, sorry about that. It'll have to be...um...the following week.
Grant	The following week. Um...Monday is— is not great for me. Um...The Tuesday would probably be— be better. Does that work for you at all?
Celia	Yes, yes, Tuesday's looking pretty free, yes. Um...I think...um...let me just check my calendar...um...for details. Um...So I think— Tuesday afternoon – is that any good?
Grant	Um...It would need to be early if possible. Perhaps about one o'clock.
Celia	Yes, sure. Just after— yes, lunchtime; that's— that's great.
Grant	Excellent! And...um...I'll come to your offices...um...as before – is that right?
Celia	Yes. That would be— that would be great. That would be really helpful.
Grant	Excellent. So...um...so just to reconfirm, it's next Tuesday— sorry, it's a week on Tuesday...um...at one o'clock.
Celia	Yes, over in our offices.
Grant	Just get that into my diary there. Excellent! Thank you very much for being so flexible. That's really very good of you.
Celia	Oh, no problem. I— I look forward to seeing you then, Grant.
Grant	Excellent. Take care. See you soon, bye now.
Celia	OK, bye bye.

Unit 10   Business hospitality

Track 27

The best way to make a good relationship between Japanese people is drink wi— together with them. Because...uh...in— in company— in office time— o— office hour, our relationship is very formal. But— but after that, we go to drink together. It is unformal situation. And in that situation Japanese people show real, real personality and...uh...drinking. So we call it *nominication*. Its mean, *nomi* means 'drink', *cation* 'communication' so *nomination* is very important for Japanese. Um... And we create a good relationship. After that...uh...they accept a solution...uh...new suggestion or different way to...uh...to do work. But before build relationship between the colleague, it is very rude attitude. So...uh...most important thing is build good relationship for drinking, I guess. I think so. Because...uh...I— I think...uh...for Western country people, it is difficult to understand the real personality of the boss or colleague of Japanese, because...um...Japanese people doesn't show— don't show their real op— opinion or real characteristic of them. Um...We— we hide the real opinion, real— real character. We— we play a role in the community. Uh...We look— look carefully each other – 'How— how do they think...uh...by— for myself?' and worry about it. Um...Just look carefully...uh...read the mood is most important thing. So...uh...aft— it is impor— Therefore, it is important to drink together and know the real character and goo— make goo— good relationship.

Track 28

Occasionally, I will take a client out to lunch ... uh ... but generally no entertaining in my home or during the evenings. I would not expect that the partners would have clients or prospective clients in their home. Rather, I think they would take them out to a nice dinner and maybe some sort of entertainment, like a play or a— a football game* or— or something of— of that nature. Football games are very much a social event, the 'tailgating' ... um ... that goes on at— at football games is— is— can be quite entertaining and very much a part of the football game experience.

'Tailgating' – where— where it came— where the term came from is, imagine a pickup truck. It has, you know, the— the tailgate which is the piece on the back that you can lay down to load stuff in and out of the truck. Or you can also sit on that tailgate and drink beer and eat hotdogs and hamburgers and play games and listen to music. So the tailgate of the truck or an SUV, that's— that's where the term came from, but 'tailgating' is actually meeting up with lots of other people who have parked their cars beside each other and brought their grills and coolers and music and sometimes TVs and all the...uh...necessary accout— accoutrements, excuse me, for tailgating. It's a— lots of fun and it happens before the football game.

* Tonya is referring to 'American football' rather than 'soccer'.

Unit 11   Talking about food

Track 29

I will recommend you the Peking duck. You know, it's very delicious. It's a— it's a duck with — Um...maybe it's not very healthy, but it's— it's really very delicious. The— the— the feather of the— no, the skin of the duck— because the duck is roast, so the skin of the duck is cru— cru— crusty? Yeah, crispy. So— and— and...um...the— the flesh of the duck is— is— is roas— is roast over the duck, so it's not dried fried, like you— like you— like you think. Then you can put the meat and the skin in the like 'taco' thing and put some sauce. The sauce is a little— little s— little sweet and a little salt— salt— So...um...and then you can eat— eat it, and it's very delicious.

Track 30

Nikki	What do you miss most?
Saya	Well, basically my— my mum's home cooking. But yeah, sometimes sashimi, which is raw fish.
Rie	Mmm, really nice one.
Saya	'Cos sushi…uh…how often— how often do you eat sushi in Japan?
Rie	Quite rare.
Saya	Yeah, isn't it? But most of— most of foreign people think…um…sushi is very popular Japanese food.
Rie	Yeah!
Nikki	Yeah, before I went there I honestly thought that I would be having sushi three meals a day. I really— I really thought…
Rie	That's crazy in Japan!
Saya	It's very occasional …
Patrick	But proper sushi— sushi is really expensive.
Saya	It is, yeah.
Rie	Yeah, even in Japan.
Patrick	Whereas— but you also have cheap sushi everywhere, like in 7-Eleven, and—
Rie	Yeah, that's true, yeah.
Patrick	And the supermarket. It's everywhere. It's cheap, it's there, it's fresh and everyone …
Rie	But not really tasty.
Patrick	No, but people eat it every day. Like, especially if you think about the— the— the set meals that men buy. OK, like, they buy the set meal from 7-Eleven and it's got 'man food'. So there's— there's always lots of rice with something on the rice and then a big pile of meat and, you know, and then some sushi – always with the sushi. Like, some kind of roll or some kind of fish or something, it's always there. Always.
Saya	Well, I think it's bento— Bentos, like a lunchbox, have some like raw fish.
Nikki	Yeah, I think that's what you're talking about, isn't it?
Patrick	Yeah, bento's kind of …yeah.
Nikki	Yeah. What do you miss most about Japanese food? Or can you get it all here?
Rie	No. Like a …uh…chicken liver – raw one.

Track 31

Well, two things when you move— when you move to the US. The first one, you kind of miss the— the food and then you also miss the— miss your community. So, when it comes to food, you know— you know the hummus, the falafel, the shawarma, that kind of stuff. And the home cooking does not exist in the US. So when you move there, you try to find— 'OK, where can I buy some Middle Eastern food?' 'Where can I buy, let's say, hummus?' Or, 'Where you can find tabouleh?' Of course, it will take you some time, something like at least three to six months to try to identify places that they actually can accommodate the same food.

Track 32

When I...uh...was going into Cork Street...um...it was in the days before they put yellow lines all over the south east of London. So I could drive to Clapham and I could jump on one of those tubes from Clapham up to— in— into town and that was easy. Uh...And I wasn't living so far out then. I used to live...um...in sort of either Purley or Coulsdon or Streatham so it was— it was— it was a really easy journey. Um...But a few years ago, we decided we wanted to move out to be more in the country so we moved to, you know, to Sussex. And the idea of getting the train from there is a bit of a pain in the bum because it's a twenty, twenty-five minute walk to the station which isn't over-appealing on a wet morning. Uh...Then I've got to get a train to Victoria, then I've got to get a tube to Hammersmith, and that process is about two and a quarter hours. So it's a long time out of your day. Whereas, if I get in the car and it's a nice day and there's not too much traffic, it's probably an hour to an hour and a quarter. Yeah, there are bad days when it's an hour and a half, and when there's a tube strike it's two hours. But hey, I'm in my own space, I can listen to the radio, I can look at the Blackberry, which I probably shouldn't say that on— when I'm driving and...uh...I can...uh...I can make the odd phone call or two. So the— the commuting is— is just something I have to put up with because I don't like living in town so I really like living in the country. And I can go home at the weekends and, five minutes walk, I'm in a wood— forest, so it's really nice. So I put up with the— with the hassle of the day-to-day commute to have nice times in the evening and at the weekends and...uh...I— just— that's what I like.

It was more difficult when the kids were younger. I mean, they're seventeen and going on fifteen now so...um...they don't— they don't need so much support. When they were a lot younger then it's more difficult 'cos you— you know, you're leaving at six thirty in the morning, you're getting back at seven o'clock at night. And when they're younger, you know, at seven o'clock at the night they're either going to bed or about to go to bed. Whereas these days we go to bed and they're up watching the telly. So...um...you know, it's kind of swapped around. But it's— it— it— it's— Having a day that probably is twelve to thirteen hours when you're away from the house is— is always gonna be tricky. Uh...But it's...I— as I say, it's worth it for the fact that I can have a— a great weekend. And, you know, you're living in the country and it's – in the car – twenty minutes to get to the coast. Twenty, twenty-five minutes. So I'll sacrifice the— the daily grind for— for that.

Track 33

I understand and appreciate that the next generation coming through is less willing to contribute up to sixty hours a week during busy season. As a culture, I think the United States has a very strong work ethic in general. Obviously not everyone, but in general. I also think that strong worth— work ethic is to our demise, at times. It certainly doesn't contribute to the family unit for Mom or Dad to be working sixty hours a week and never be home for dinner for three months out of the year. That's— that's not good for us. So I think it's a positive change, I do.

Unit 13   Talking about your work

Track 34

OK, I'm responsible for the induction as well. Uh…We've got a few people down in…uh…Facilities and we do share inductions. So…um…my induction is every third Monday of— of the month. Uh…We usually get a list of new employees sent by HR…uh…so we know how many people are attending. I meet them in the HR office…uh…straight after they finish their HR and IT induction. And I take them for a walk, actually – because facilities…uh…induction is part— part of the induction is, like, a walk through the building. Uh…We talk about…uh…fire…uh…issues…uh…health and safety stuff. I take…um…new employees for a walk and show them their nearest fire exit. I explain what they can find in the kitchen in— regarding…uh…like, first aid kit, our list of fire wardens, list of firstaiders as well. I explain…um…structure of the building…um…where they can find the nearest lift, a toilet, et cetera. Uh…Then I take them down to canteen, explain what they— what they can expect in canteen. Uh…Opening hours, and then walk through the post room. And all details about post room side of the building…um…and Facilities as well.

Track 35

When I was at university, I studied Politics and…um…I did a double degree in Politics and Journalism and became— I was— I've always been interested in politics…um…but I got involved with a political party…um…back home. And through my involvement…um…landed myself a fantastic job as a junior policy adviser for a Government minister – so a state minister. Um…And I absolutely loved it. It— it was something that, you know, had my blood pumping every single day. And it's very exciting to, sort of, know things before they hit the news. Um…There's always something dramatic going on, there's always some sort of back-stabbing, always affairs. It's— you know, it's an incredibly interesting…um…world in which these people live. And they live it 24 hours a day, which, I think, was one of the reasons why I felt that it may not be something I wanted to do long-term. And there is quite a high burn-out rate. Um…And I— I guess I sort of felt that it would always be there if I wanted to go back to it. Um…But, as a young person, you get put under a lot of pressure to, sort of…uh…be quite engaged and do as much as you can for the party and also think about your— your own personal ambitions and try and, you know, there's a lot of lining up that happens, and grooming and all that sort of stuff. So…um…so I just felt that it— I— To be really honest, I just felt that I was becoming a person who I didn't really like. And I felt like I wasn't necessarily true to myself. And I felt that it was an industry that you, sort of, had to not have that many morals or ethical expectations of yourself.

Um…So— But having said that, absolutely phenomenal first job to have. I mean, it has let— allowed me to— Um…You have to have a certain sort of work ethic to work in a political office, you know, and you always have to roll your sleeves up and get in and do some hard yakka…um…that may not be glamorous, that, you know, you might be well overpaid for – but it doesn't matter. Um…So it's given me a great wor— work ethic and also I think it has trained me in a certain way of problem-solving and thinking about…um…thinking about situations in a very different way.

Unit 14   Finance and accounting

Track 36

I'm studying for CIMA, or— it's the Chartered Institute of Management Accountancy, which is a global…um…body that looks after CIMA-qualified accountants. But there's also ACA and ACCA and they…um…are financial accountants. They would be more focused on…uh…balance sheets and…um…P&Ls. That's what you would have to be to be an auditor. It's quite outwardly focussed, so it would be if you were presenting accounts to shareholders or…um…external people – stakeholders in general. And there are strict guidelines of how these accounts have to be presented and the way things within them have to be accounted for. A management accountant normally is more internally focused so will work with managing directors…um…CEOs or just management within a division…um…looking at things like controlling costs, how to get the best out of things, how to better manage things internally to get the best outcome that you can have while operating the business, other than presenting stuff externally under, sort of, strict guidelines.

Track 37

I work within the management accountancy team, so all of us here are management accountants. There's a separate division within our company that looks after…um…the purchase ledger, the cash flow – and they all work in a different city. So, we have contact with them over the phone, talking about…um…what's sitting on our balance sheet,…um…how our P&L's coming together. But they look after the nitty-gritty of actually putting the accruals, looking after the general ledger. Um…But there will be— within the account— Our FD would be looking after not only the management accountancy part but he will also be looking after the people that are purchasing currency, the people that are making the transactions up in the…um…call centre that take orders. He'll be looking after such a broad range – once you're that senior, you'll be doing a whole lot of accounts stuff that I only do a small part of.

Track 38

I am a CPA in public practice. I work with a small accounting firm. Um … They employ less than a hundred people. Um … My day-to-day activities as an accountant involve … um … reviewing financial statements and ensuring that my department is complying with all the applicable … uh … accounting standards and laws and regulations. Um … I do a good bit of research – accounting research – to ensure that all transactions are recorded properly and reported in the financial statements properly. And I also do some training for our firm.

I've been in my current role for just over three years. Prior to that, I worked with … um … a large publicly-traded Fortune 500 company and … uh … my role there was as an internal auditor. Just before that, I was in public practice as an auditor – an external auditor – independent auditor.

Unit 15   Parental leave and redundancy

Track 39

The situation with maternity leave in the UK is that you have the right to keep your job open – your job has to be kept open for you by your employer for 12 months. You're not paid for that whole time. Um…I think the statutory— currently the statutory maternity leave is something like 6 weeks at 90% of your salary. And then there's something called…um…statutory maternity pay which is very low – much, much lower than most people's salaries. And that's just a, sort of, small contribution for the rest of the— the rest of the time. And I think you're allowed that for the following 9 months or so. So if you take the full 12 months there is a financial sacrifice but you do have the right to go back to your original job or your— an equivalent job in the same organisation.

Paternity leave, I believe, is two weeks. Um…I think it's at 90% of pay but most companies just give you two weeks' extra holiday. And that can be taken at any time – it doesn't have to be at the birth of the baby. Most people I know take the two weeks and then they add some of their annual leave on top, so they end up taking three weeks or a month off work if they can.

Track 40

At the time when— So my— my children are aged nine and— and eleven – two sons. Um …… At that time when…um…my wife…uh…who, at that time, worked for the same company…um…went off on maternity leave…um…fathers weren't gifted the same paternity rights as they are currently. So at that time, I think I had one or two days' …uh…paternity leave. Uh…The rest of the time I took off as— as ordinary annual leave…um…but no paternity leave as such.

I think it is an improvement in the system that men…uh…do gain— gain paternity rights. Um…I don't think they…uh…should get equal treatment as the mother is, you know, off on maternity leave look— looking after…uh …the children, kind of, longer term. But it's all a question of choice and it may suit—…uh…it may suit some families better that the— that the father is— has gained equal rights…uh…as the mother. Um…In my personal circumstances…uh…it wouldn't have affected me otherwise because at the time of having… uh…my children, you know, we had already arranged for my— my wife to come back to— back to work. Uh …. We'd a— lined up adequate…uh…childcare and that had always been part of her plan when we were—…uh…arranging to plan a family and— and have kids.

Track 41

I was made redundant last year and it was a bit of a shock. I happened to be on maternity leave at the time. I was told that it was likely to happen and the difficult thing for me was that it was gonna happen just at the time that I was due to go back to work, or I had told the company that I was planning on going back to work. It wasn't a total surprise, given some of the things that had been happening in the company in— in the previous year or two. But the speed at which it happened was— was quite a surprise. So, I got a phone call at home from my boss' boss who wasn't based in the UK – he was actually based in Asia. And he told me that this process was going on, and that the reason I was facing redundancy was that my company was being bought by another one, which had been under discussion for a while but because I was out of the office, I didn't know about it. And I think it was only— it was perhaps three or four weeks after that initial conversation that the whole thing was formalised and I…uh…I was made redundant. And when I first got told it was likely to happen, I was very worried about it because, as I said, I was coming back from my maternity leave. I knew that we were in a recession – a very bad recession – at exactly that time, and I really had no idea of the— the health of the other companies that I might work for.

So what actually happened was that I had a really good excuse to contact all my contacts, let people know what had happened, that I was looking for work and I got in touch with some people I hadn't got in touch with for years, got a— I got a really good understanding of what was happening in— in my field. I got to go in for interviews with quite a few of our competitors, who I— I knew— knew of and I knew about, but I hadn't actually ever gone into their buildings and met some of the top people there. And things worked out really well. I— I got the freelance contract almost immediately through that networking and I was headhunted for a role – the role I'm currently in – which is actually probably my favourite job to date, and one that…um…I'm very pleased to be in. So, all in all, quite a positive experience.

Unit 16   Planning a business trip

Track 42

The success of any business trip…uh…especially where there are back-to-back…uh…schedules and meetings over various locations needed – is in the preparation. Um…In the case of this trip…uh…which was a two week— extended over a two week period, as I said – I think the preparation and meetings were teed up over the course of four weeks, trying to coordinate everyone's availability in the various cities and even districts to cut down on travelling time. Um…In addition to that…um…and to make the trip as meaningful as possible, and to speed up the way in which you can assess…uh…the abilities of prospective suppliers and partners. …um…there were standard documentation packs which were produced. These were produced by myself…uh…in some parts. I had the assistance of…um…an assistant— of a PA…um…Michelle, who…um…coordinated all the main schedules in relation to the supplier visits. I had technical packs created by…um…my Product Support Manager. He's pulled together all of the necessary data. So there was a combined team effort…uh…which took place over— from about four, maybe even six weeks in some cases, in advance of…uh…visiting the suppliers, and there was a comprehensive schedule…uh…lined up.

That being said, there was still one problem! Uh…There was…uh…Of— of the dozens of meetings which were attended there was one…um…meeting which should've gone ahead. Uh…And we were driving up and down…um…the main road in India – it was in Chennai – looking for a premises and…through no fault of anyone's – other than the suppliers themselves – they had actually recently moved premises! So all of the email literature, the instructions that they'd provided in terms of where to visit and the time…um…you know…uh…it was all irrelevant because we were in the wrong place at the right time. You know, unfortunately it turns out, when we eventually…uh…tried to phone them, even the phone numbers were out of date. They eventually…uh…called us…um…to say 'Are you coming for your meeting?' and we told them where we were – if they could ask for directions and…uh…it turned— turned out they were…um…two hours outside the city that we were in itself! Anyway, these things happen and we have to reschedule the appointment for another time in the UK.

Track 43

Well…um…working with the Middle Eastern markets was really, really interesting…um…not least because you— you're dealing with lots of— with a different culture, essentially. And…um…you have to take into considera— consideration stuff like…um…that they— they work over there Sunday to Thursday, so I had to time my trips accordingly. So it— you know, it's just being aware of cultural sensitivities…um…and making sure that you adapt yourself…um…within that context to— to communicate effectively to the people you are working with, and being respectful of that.

So when I travelled to the UAE, it was…um…for week-long trips. I'd be based in London throughout…um…and then go over there for about a week. Um…Sometimes I'd try and tag on a couple of territories such as…um…the UAE…um…and then…uh…nip to Beirut afterwards. But that would generally take me about 10 days…um…which was the longest trip I ever did.

Unit 17   Cross-cultural negotiation

Track 44

Japanese people think…uh…insist their opinion is a very rude attitude for colleague, oth— other colleague. For example…uh…the boss order some works for Western country people, but they…uh…they don't want to do that. Uh…They suggest another so— solution or another way to…uh…work that things. But it is very rude for Japanese, because…uh…for Japanese, Japanese culture has a Confucianism so we should obey the— the elder people. Uh…Mainly the boss is much older than…uh…the businessmen…so if…suggest another solution, it is good for business but it is bad for relationship. So, sometimes…um…Western people insist their— their opinion, show their opinion different way, is rude and…uh…the boss feels co— uncomfortable for that attitude. So it is difficult to adjust— adjust…uh…Western people…I guess.

Track 45

I would say if I have to describe business…um…to…Far East Asian people…um…Chinese or Japanese…uh…I would…um…describe the way business is conducted…uh…in France as…uh…quite dynamic…um…with people that like…um…to argument and to explain and…um…before making a decision to…um…to challenge a little bit…um…opinions of people. So it could be sometimes perceived as a bit intrusive or a bit rude…uh…which it's not. Uh…I would say if somebody care of what you're doing and…um…care of…um…your…um…your opinion, he will probably challenge you and ask you a lot of question.…um…which is something that you need to— to understand and to expect as something positive rather than something negative.

Track 46

As far as I…um…working as legal consultant in…uh…I mean, a big company, we have a lot of chance to— chances to negotiate wi— negotiate with different companies…uh…such as in— in the UK or in the— in the…um…in America. And some is local company. I think the negotiating style is…uh…a li— a little different. For example, if— if we negotiate with…uh…Japanese company, they are quite…uh…emphasise on the…uh…on every wor— on every word and…uh…every detail— details. Yeah, it's…uh … You will find…um…we have to spend a lot of time on the details. Um…Every detail they will, if they don't— it don't…uh…make sure that they will need to confirm at their headquarter or legal consult because sometimes we negotiate with their market department…uh…or sales department. So, it's quite— it quite be very long. But…uh…in local people— in local company such as in some Chinese company…uh…it will be push— we will be pushed very fast. Because in China, sometimes maybe some company don't emphasise on the legal too much, so— so much, so they prefer finish this project soon— as soon as possible.

Track 47

I send a lot of emails out to people in Taiwan and China and Hong Kong …uh …Asia – lots of …uh …where there's lots of consumer electronics industries based. What I've found, when I get my responses back from them, is that grammar and spelling of— of English is just not as important for them when they're writing emails. Like, I feel like you— you kind of— you get a lot more loose in your— in your tolerance for …uh …correct forms of English. You kinda have to just accept that people have a very, I dunno, a looser understanding of things, and you know, you find yourself not really under— You know, you read a sentence and you don't read the literal meaning of it. Uh …You just kind of need to interpret it to see what they're getting at because they …um …I mean, they're using words so differently.

I got this email from this woman and she signed it 'Chi Chi', right? And she signed it with a signature – like an image signature – and above the— the I's were little hearts so it was Chi Chi with two hearts. That's how she signed a business email, you know? Like, I just, I just don't think over on this side of the world – the Western world – that you would sign emails with emoticons. Uh …It's a cultural thing, I guess. It's not that it's a bad thing. It's kind of friendly, I guess …just strange.

Track 48

So during the business maybe we have some misunderstanding …um …between the foreign countries. For example, we— sometimes we have to write email or telephone the foreign countries. Um …I remember …um …once I called a …uh …manager in German. Because …um …his English maybe is not very …um …very good because he's not English native speaker, so his …um …pronunciation maybe is hard for me to understand. Um …But …uh …then we— we …um …we think— we— we— maybe it's better for us to write down the words in em— email. We can find the words and refer to the dictionary and to find out the exact meaning what he said.

Track 49

Um …My direct manager …um …is based in London and I'm based in Glasgow. Um …And there are a few constraints in that we don't have face-to-face meetings on a daily basis, but both of us travel up and down …um …perhaps once a month or so. And we can communicate by phone, instant messaging and email. Um …I think it's important to keep up that level of communication when there's a distance there. But it— in the long run it doesn't really set us back any and I think …um …as long as …um …people are willing to travel …um …then I— I see no problem with it.

Again, working with …um …external agencies globally …um …I think it's important to …um …to travel every so often to see customers and to see— to see agencies face-to-face as it— it solidifies the partnership and the relationship there. And it really— I think it makes a good impression for the customer's point of view.

Unit 19   Meeting and greeting

Track 50

Well, in Spain, when you meet someone – even when you meet someone for the first time – if it's, like, friend of friend, you could kiss them on the cheek, you know, and— twice. But if you're meeting someone for the first time and it's, you know, in a business environment, you're not gonna kiss them on the cheek – you're gonna shake hands. And maybe after some times you— you get to actually kiss them on the cheeks, but not at the beginning. And…um…I know…um…it— you know, for foreigners who go to Spain, at the beginning they— some of them are shocked a little bit. But with the time I have seen it, you know, they get used to it and they really like it. And I think it's because, you know, we are open and for us…um…feeling, touching someone is very important. So yeah. But I have actually noticed that people kiss in both cheeks, you know, more and more in London. And I think it's because also the— the— the mix of nationalities. It's not only, you know, Spain, Italians, or— they also do this kind of…uh…greetings. Um…And then, yeah, the huggings. Maybe— maybe the hugging's more when you know the people, you know, after a certain time.

Track 51

I think Italian people is really people with a good fantasy – happy people. We enjoy to be together, to organise also dinner— restaurants together – we are really easy-going people. But sometimes, for people from other countries, those things could be too much because they are not used to us. And, for example, I am from the south of Italy. For me, it's common to— when I meet a friend, just to hug and to kiss him or her. Doesn't matter if it's a boy or it's a girl. But in this country, if I kiss one guy, for example, just a friend, people can think something about my sexual orientation and for me it's really strange! I need to hide myself and to block— to lock myself. I cannot express myself in one hundred per cents – totally.

Track 52

When my colleagues have to go to the Middle East, for example…um…there are little things that they need to remember, like a lot of females work in our office, so most of the team is actually female. Um…And when they go to the Middle East, for example…um…they're not supposed to shake hands with the men that they meet. And, of course, in the Middle East most…um…most of the working world is dominated by men. So a lot of the customers that they deal with – all of their clients – tend to be typically male. Um…So there are a lot of cultural things like that that they've— they've gotta deal with and— and remember when they go abroad. Um…Alternatively there…um…there are little— just the little nuances of— of business culture in Asia, for example – handing over a business card with two hands. Um…You know, it's quite rude to hand over a business card with one hand, as we do in— in the Western world.

Unit 20   Working hours and the office environment

Track 53

The working hours depends on the kind of business. Um…It's one thing I don't like about, you know, certain kind of business in Spain like …uh …travel agencies …um …or even office …um …working hours – because of the siesta, you know. They— Normally, they used to work maybe eight to one or something like that, or eight to twelve and then you have one or two hours for lunch and then you had to go back to the office and work until maybe seven. I don't like that. I prefer working, you know, eight hours in a row with half an hour break – something like that. So that's one of the things that maybe they would say that a little bit strange.

I— I think they would prefer working the eight hours in a row because you finish early and you have the rest of the day, you know, for yourself or your family or for whatever you want to do. Um …But, as I say, it depends on the business that you're in. Or if you work in a hotel, that's fine. You do a shift and work either quite early in the morning, then you finish at three in the afternoon, or you do a late shift which leaves you the morning free for yourself so.

Track 54

My office is shared in two parts: one half is— is totally and full Japanese and the second half is the Italian island plus Spanish, Polish and German island. So half of our office is really quiet; everything is clean and tidy. The second half is like the hells. So it's— just imagine the Dante's Hells. Open the door, look at your left: wow, heaven! Look at your right: there is the hells! People chatting, walking …But we are really— at the end of the months we are really productive so this is no matter. And also our manager is half Italian, half Colombian but he— he grew up in UK. He is English but his roots are half Italian, half Colombian so he is really a Latin man – a Latin guy. He manages to organise the office in that way. Everyone is happy, everyone is smiling in the office and we are enjoying what we are doing. But the other half of the office is quite sad. You can also hear in the— just the sound of one fly moving in the air …and in our second— in our half you cannot hear the sound of a storm outside because we are the storm inside. So I think you can understand which kind of office, but it's really professional office.

I think the Japanese part is quiet because for their culture they have to hide the emotion inside. I— I lived for two years in Italy with a Japanese guy and six months in Portugal with a Japanese girl. And during also the private life they were behaving in the same way. And my friends, the Japanese guy I used to live in Italy with, one day told me, 'We are just having a— a party outside.' It was really serious. I— I asked him 'Is everything OK, are you feel well?' 'Oh yeah, yeah, I'm really happy!' And I asked 'Why you are not showing that – this happiness?' And he replied me, 'Outside I'm quite— I'm— I look calm and relaxed but inside I'm jumping and partying.' So from that moment I understood that from their culture they need to hide the emotion inside – they need to keep the emotion inside. They are happy but they don't show the happiness they have. And Italian people is totally the opposite.

Track 55

Uh …Basically at the moment we have …uh …two girls that work part-time – so one comes in at seven o'clock in the morning and she leaves at eight o'clock— at eleven o'clock. And the other one picks up where she leaves off, so she comes in at eleven and she leaves at four. And then I— myself, I work from eight until five-fifteen, same as Carl who comes in at seven until about four-thirty, five o'clock. And then the chefs, they come in at seven until about three-thirty – as soon as lunch is finished and they've cleaned up and everything's spick and span and then they off.